THE ULTIMATE BOOK OF
DINOSAURS

UNION
SQUARE
kids

NEW YORK

CONTENTS

THE AGE OF REPTILES	8
TIMELINE	12
THE WORLD OF DINOSAURS	14
HOW TO READ THE DIAGRAMS	18

CARNIVOROUS DINOSAURS

INTRODUCTION 20	**TROODON** 52
IN THE FOOTSTEPS OF PREDATORS 22	**ALLOSAURUS** 56
DEINONYCHUS 24	**CERATOSAURUS** 62
GUANLONG 26	**ICHTHYOVENATOR** 64
DILOPHOSAURUS 28	**SPINOSAURUS** 66
CARNOTAURUS 30	**BARYONYX** 70
MICRORAPTOR 34	**AUSTRORAPTOR** 74
CITIPATI 36	**ACROCANTHOSAURUS** 78
GIGANOTOSAURUS 38	**GALLIMIMUS** 82
VELOCIRAPTOR 42	**TYRANNOSAURUS** 84
OVIRAPTOR 48	**ARCHAEOPTERYX** 90

HERBIVOROUS DINOSAURS

INTRODUCTION		94		STYGIMOLOCH	140
HERBIVORES' TEETH		96		MAIASAURA	142
	ALAMOSAURUS	98		ANKYLOSAURUS	146
	PUERTASAURUS	102		ARGENTINOSAURUS	150
	TRICERATOPS	104		PARASAUROLOPHUS	154
	TOROSAURUS	108		OURANOSAURUS	158
	EINIOSAURUS	112		AMARGASAURUS	160
	DIABLOCERATOPS	116		PLATEOSAURUS	164
	PROTOCERATOPS	120		LAMBEOSAURUS	166
	PACHYRHINOSAURUS	126		THERIZINOSAURUS	168
	DIPLODOCUS	130		STEGOSAURUS	170
	APATOSAURUS	134		ALTIRHINUS	174
	PACHYCEPHALOSAURUS	136		IGUANODON	176

PTEROSAURS

INTRODUCTION	182	**RHAMPHORHYNCHUS**	196
QUETZALCOATLUS	184	**TAPEJARA**	200
PTERANODON	188	**TUPANDACTYLUS**	202
PTERODACTYLUS	194	**EUDIMORPHODON**	204

MARINE REPTILES

INTRODUCTION	208	**ICHTHYOSAURUS**	222
STENOPTERYGIUS	210	**PLIOSAURUS**	224
TYLOSAURUS	214	**PLESIOSAURUS**	226
ELASMOSAURUS	216	**LIOPLEURODON**	228
MOSASAURUS	218		

EXTINCTION	230	**ALPHABETICAL ORDER OF DINOSAURS**	238
THEME PARKS AND MUSEUMS	234	**IMAGE CREDITS**	238
GLOSSARY	236	**AUTHORS**	240

The boldfaced terms throughout the text are defined in the glossary

THE AGE OF REPTILES

The history of life on Earth includes periods when both animals and plants flourished, and times when the various forms of life experienced sudden changes in the environments they had conquered. Those changes were often due to catastrophic events that caused life forms to eventually disappear.

Indeed, 252 million years ago, life was almost erased from Earth. The living creatures that managed to survive found themselves in an almost empty world, with new environments to spread into and develop in. This was the beginning of what **paleontologists**, or scientists who study fossils, call the Mesozoic **era**. This name means "middle life," and it was chosen because the life forms that inhabited Earth at that time were different from both those of the past and those that exist today. The Mesozoic is often referred to as the "Age of Reptiles." It was, in fact, the reptiles that had the greatest advantages for filling the void left in the world, and they conquered all three environments: land, water, and air.

Plateosaurus was a Triassic herbivore with short front legs.

TRIASSIC

The Mesozoic Era is divided into three periods: Triassic, Jurassic, and Cretaceous.

In the Triassic **period** (251.9–201.3 million years ago), the landmasses of the world were still bound together into the supercontinent of **Pangaea**. The climate was pretty hot and dry, except in the coastal areas, thanks to the humidity from the sea. The environments were therefore mostly desert, especially those a long way from the coast. The main plants were conifers (relatives of today's pines and firs), tree ferns, and a few varieties of ginkgo. In the late Triassic period, 230 million years ago, the first dinosaurs appeared on land, the first marine reptiles appeared in the ocean, and the first pterosaurs appeared in the sky. **Mammals** also developed, although they were no bigger than a small dog. Toward the end of the Triassic, Pangaea began to split apart, and the ocean started filling the area between the two new continents.

JURASSIC

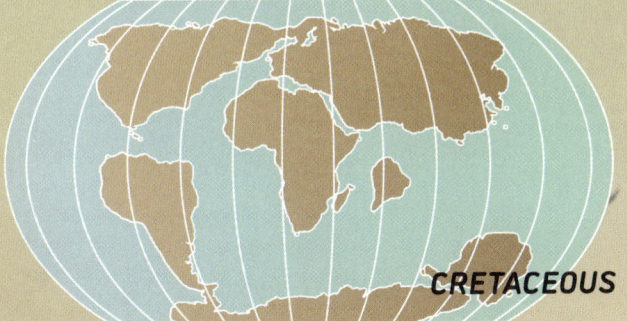
CRETACEOUS

TODAY

This extinction event was one of five that marked the beginning of the Jurassic period (201–145 million years ago). The climate remained hot, but it gradually became more and more humid, allowing plants to spread easily across the land and the animals that fed on them to change and develop. Not only were there reptiles everywhere during the Jurassic, but it was also the period in which the dinosaurs became the largest animals to ever walk on our planet. Large sauropods (or long-necked dinosaurs) like *Apatosaurus* and *Diplodocus* developed and fed on vast forests of gymnosperms, such as conifers, ginkgoes, and cycads.

The herbivores were followed by carnivores, which also grew to substantial sizes, such as *Allosaurus* and *Ceratosaurus*. The evolution of the smaller dinosaurs, on the other hand, led to the birth of the first avian dinosaurs—that is, birds.

Dinosaurs reached their peak during the Cretaceous period (145–66 million years ago), with the appearance of species like *Tyrannosaurus*, *Spinosaurus*, and *Triceratops*. Giant *Elasmosaurus* and mosasaurs swam in the oceans. Flying reptiles such as *Quetzalcoatlus* were the largest animals ever to take to the sky, although they had to share it with the birds that were already widespread during this period. But it was also the period that saw the end of these incredible reptiles.

At the end of the Cretaceous, there was another catastrophe. Just as the dinosaurs had risen due to the events that had almost destroyed the life forms before them in the Paleozoic era, this one would lead to their fall.

the first marine vertebrates appear

land plants appear

the first reptiles appear

amphibians appear

EPOCH

PERIOD

CAMBRIAN | ORDOVICIAN | SILURIAN | DEVONIAN | CARBONIFEROUS | PERMIAN

ERA

PALEOZOIC

EON

PHANEROZOIC

AGE MILLION YEARS AGO: 541.0 | 485.4 | 443.8 | 419.2 | 358.9 | 298.9

TIMELINE

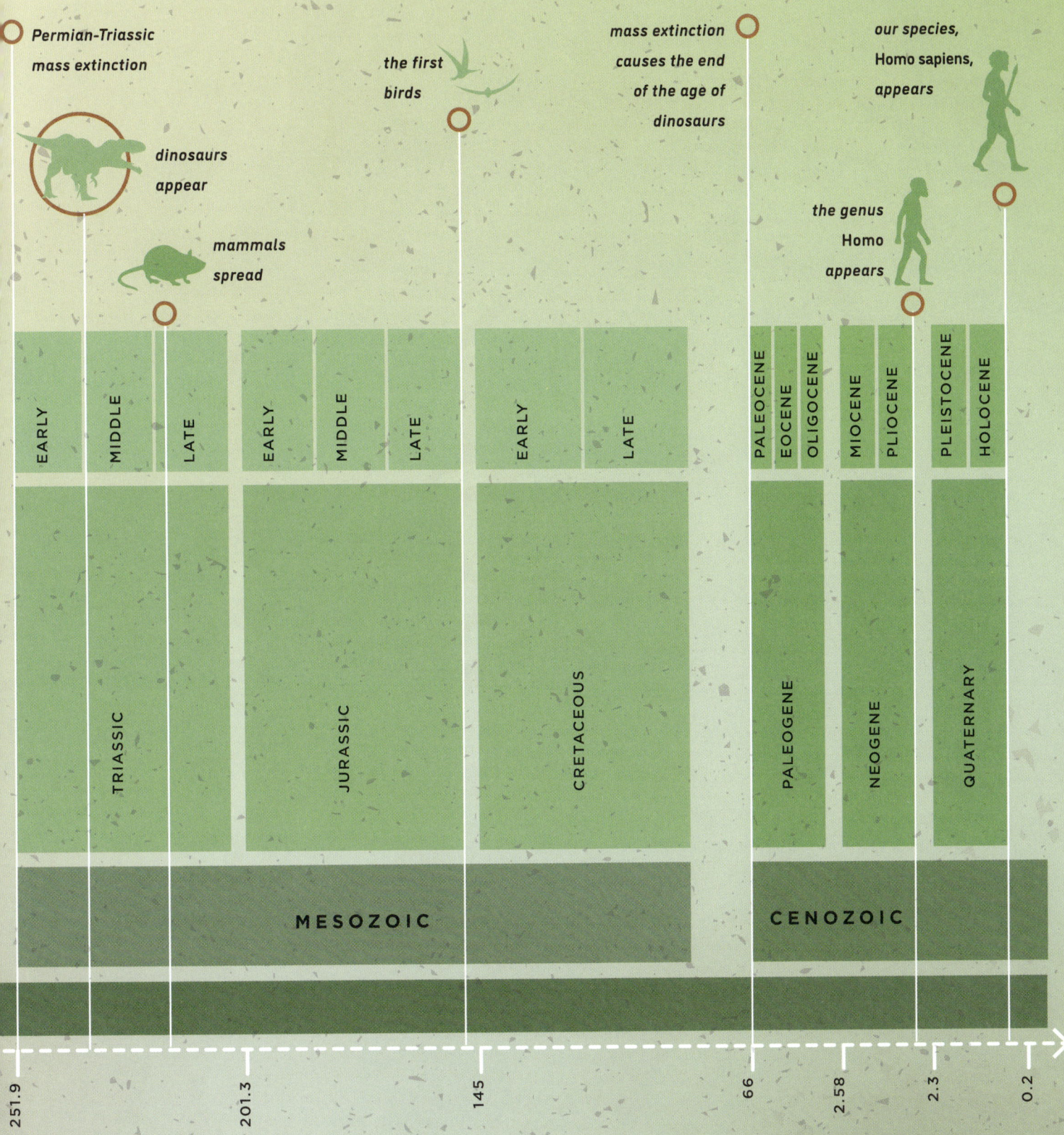

THE WORLD OF DINOSAURS

Dinosaurs were a very diverse group of reptiles: some were as small as pigeons, while others were giants, even bigger than a truck. The main characteristic that dinosaurs had in common was the position and structure of their limbs. Unlike other reptiles, most **dinosaurs** had limbs that were straight and upright under the body, like columns. Their skin was protected by **scales**, and some parts were covered in plumage or feathers.

Their brains were relatively small for their body size, and in some cases, they were truly tiny. Despite this, they ruled Earth for about 150 million years. Considering that our species, Homo sapiens, only appeared 300,000 years ago, that's a really long time.

In the past, dinosaurs were considered very clumsy, slow, and not very intelligent animals, perhaps due to the small size of their brains. However, today they are understood differently, mainly by comparing them with their living descendants, birds, which are now considered living dinosaurs.

Like birds, dinosaurs were probably able to maintain a constant body temperature. Paleontologists have found evidence to support this theory by analyzing the fossilized shells of their eggs. The shells contain substances that tell us the temperature of the place where they formed—that is, in the body of the female dinosaur. Thanks to these studies, we know that the body temperature of dinosaurs was similar to that of today's birds and higher than that of the environment they lived in.

The first dinosaurs were small, agile, and bipedal (or walked on two feet), but during the Triassic they evolved into very different forms. Most of them became plant-eating dinosaurs, while a few became formidable hunters. The oldest dinosaur **fossils**, like those of *Eoraptor* or *Pisanosaurus*, were discovered in Argentina and are about 230 million years old. These were the first discovered remains from the groups Saurischia (carnivores and giant long-necked quadrupeds) and **Ornithischia** (all other plant eaters).

BIRTH OF A NAME

The first dinosaur to be described scientifically was *Megalosaurus*, in 1824, followed by *Iguanodon* a year later. But these animals weren't yet called "dinosaurs." The term was coined in 1842 by the English paleontologist Richard Owen, who combined two Greek terms to convey how amazed he was by these extraordinary animals: *deinos* (which means both "wonderful" and "terrible") and *sauros* ("reptile" or "lizard").

Styracosaurus

HOW TO READ THE DIAGRAMS

ITS WEIGHT:

maximum 2 tons (1814 kg)

The circle represents the weight of the dinosaur compared to an adult person who weighs about 176 lb. (80 kg)

ITS SIZE:

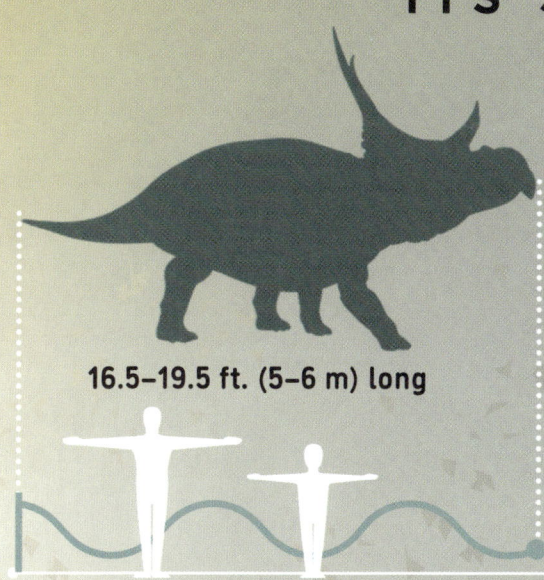

16.5–19.5 ft. (5–6 m) long

The green line represents the length of the dinosaur and is compared to the size of an adult person and a child

CARNIVOROUS D

The name means MEAT EATERS

THESE DINOSAURS' MAIN WEAPONS WERE THEIR TEETH AND CLAWS

The first carnivorous, or meat-eating, dinosaurs emerged in the Triassic. They were small and had a light build. However, many different forms developed soon after, and in the middle of the Jurassic, between 200 and 165 million years ago, there were several large carnivores. But the biggest and most famous predators, like *Tyrannosaurus*, *Spinosaurus*, and *Giganotosaurus*, didn't appear until the Cretaceous, the last period of the Mesozoic.

They used a variety of hunting techniques. Very large dinosaurs used their size to terrorize and defeat the competition. Others would **ambush** their prey, or hide and wait before attacking. Small and agile dinosaurs depended on their speed. These dinosaurs' main weapons were their teeth and **claws**. Much of the information we have about dinosaurs comes from their teeth, which were constantly replaced. Their teeth stayed pointed, sharp, and sometimes also serrated, which means jagged like a knife—ideal for killing prey and ripping off chunks of meat. They were, however, useless for chewing.

In fact, carnivorous dinosaurs swallowed their food whole since they weren't able to move their mouth in the side-to-side motion needed for chewing. The jaws, on the other hand, had to be strong, with large muscles for a very powerful bite. Most of them were bipedal, and they used their long tails to balance the weight of their large, heavy heads. Most of these dinosaurs had hands that were useful for grabbing, wounding, and holding down prey during combat, and this is why they had claws that were strong, curved, and sharp.

Some of them had particularly long, feathered limbs, which were also used to provide protection and warmth to the eggs during brooding. Others, like *Carnotaurus* and *Tyrannosaurus*, had very short arms, which were useless for hunting—in fact, these dinosaurs only used their mouth to hold down and kill their prey.

Many carnivorous dinosaurs, both small and large, were covered in plumage and feathers, which according to paleontologists were very colorful. The feathers had many functions: smaller dinosaurs needed them to keep warm, or, in a few rare cases, to fly, while larger dinosaurs probably used them for **display** during **mating rituals**.

NOSAURS

IN THE FOOTSTEPS OF PREDATORS

Fossil bones are like an incomplete photograph of the dinosaur they belonged to. Fossilized footprints, on the other hand, are like a movie: they tell us how the dinosaur moved, at what speed, how it walked, and whether it lived alone or in a group. For example, footprints have made it possible to learn that dinosaurs did not rest their tails on the ground while walking.

A single footprint doesn't provide a lot of information, but a trail of three or more footprints in a row, left by the same animal, provides a treasure trove of information and helps to solve certain mysteries.

For example, footprint trails make it possible to determine the speed of the animal that left them. Footprints that are close together tell us that it was walking, but if they are far apart, we can assume the dinosaur was running. Was it chasing prey or fleeing danger?

It is not usually possible to identify the dinosaur that left the footprints, as they are almost never found near the remains of its skeleton. The **fossilization** process for bones is different from the one that preserves footprints.

However, in some cases it is possible to hypothesize which animal left them. The shape and size of the footprints are compared with the limbs of all the species of dinosaurs discovered in the same area, helping to find possible candidates for the footprints. This is why different types of footprints are given their own name and not that of the animal that left them. Fossilized footprints are **trace fossils,** along with eggs and coprolites, which are fossilized dung.

Detail of an *Allosaurus* handprint

Eubrontes   *Grallator*   *Dromaeopodus*

Carnivores had four toes on their feet, although most of the time only three touched the ground. Many different types of dinosaur footprints have been found, all with elongated toes and claws. Those known as Eubrontes are large and have massive toes. Grallator footprints are medium to small and are characterized by a very elongated middle toe. Dromaeopodus footprints only show two toes and were a mystery for a long time, since none of the dinosaurs had only two toes on their feet. However, today paleontologists think these footprints were left by dinosaurs similar to Velociraptor, which held its large-clawed toe off the ground when it walked, and so it isn't visible in its footprint. *Tyrannosauripus* footprints are enormous, over 27 inches (70 cm) long, and often show the **print** of the toe that was usually held off the ground.

DEINON

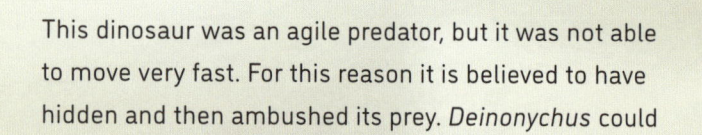

This dinosaur was an agile predator, but it was not able to move very fast. For this reason it is believed to have hidden and then ambushed its prey. *Deinonychus* could climb trees, and it would attack its prey by leaping onto it and holding it down with its powerful arms and sharp teeth.

It used its famous sickle claw, which was about 6 inches (15 cm) long, to climb trees, but it was also a powerful weapon for pinning down or wounding its victims. This claw was held off the ground when the dinosaur walked or ran, so it was always sharp and in perfect condition.

DISTINCTIVE FEATURES: a large claw on the second toe of each foot

YCHUS

Its name means:
TERRIBLE CLAW

WHERE IT LIVED:

North America

ITS WEIGHT:

154–220 lb.
(70–100 kg)

ITS SIZE:

up to 11 ft. (3.4 m) long

WHEN IT LIVED:

115–106 million years ago

TRIASSIC | JURASSIC | CRETACEOUS

THE REBIRTH OF THE DINOSAURS

The discovery of *Deinonychus* sparked a revolution among paleontologists known as the **Dinosaur Renaissance**. This changed the way scientists thought about carnivorous dinosaurs: they weren't just large, awkward, and ungainly reptiles—they were also fast and agile predators.

IT SHOULD HAVE BEEN A MOVIE STAR

Deinonychus was a victim of "identity theft" when it was used as a model for the *Velociraptor* in the *Jurassic Park* movies. The director thought that *Velociraptors* were too small to be scary enough and decided to use their bigger relatives. So why didn't he call them by their correct name? Simple: he thought viewers would prefer the name *Velociraptor*.

GUANLO

Guanlong was a small dinosaur that was related to one of the largest and most famous predators of all time: *Tyrannosaurus rex*. It was discovered in 2002 among some rocks in the Chinese region of Xinjiang. Today there are only two almost-complete skeletons, found one on top of the other, just a few inches apart. The first—the one found closer to the surface—is of a 12-year-old adult, while the second specimen, or sample that was found, is of a 6-year-old juvenile, not yet mature.

DISTINCTIVE FEATURES: a very thin crest

N G

Its name means:
CROWNED DRAGON

WHERE IT LIVED:

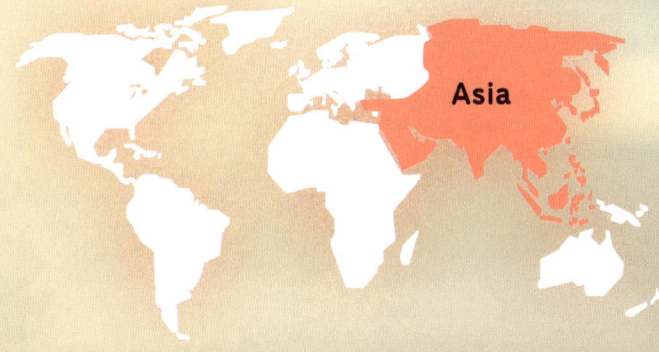

Asia

Guanlong is the oldest known tyrannosaurid. It had some similar characteristics to its larger and more recent relatives, but there are a few differences: it had long arms, each with three fingers that were useful for holding down prey, and a very well-developed crest that ran along the entire snout, from the nostrils to the eye sockets. *Guanlong* was an agile hunter that hunted in a forest environment and could feed on small to medium-sized animals, but it was prey to other larger carnivores that shared its habitat, similar to allosaurs, which would definitely have been able to hunt it.

ITS WEIGHT:

200 lb. (90 kg)

ITS SIZE:

10 ft. (3 m) long

WHEN IT LIVED:

159–154 million years ago

| TRIASSIC | JURASSIC | CRETACEOUS |

THE CREST

The main distinctive, or unique, feature of this small tyrannosaur was the crest in the center of the **skull**, which curved toward the back of the head.

The discovery of two specimens of different ages made it possible to determine that the crest was less developed in juveniles. An adult's crest was about 2.4 inches (6 cm) high and over 6 inches (15 cm) long, but it was very thin, so it was highly unlikely to have been used as a weapon. Scholars believe that the crest may have been very colorful and therefore used for mating displays and recognizing other *Guanlongs*.

DILOPHO

A narrow snout, delicate bones, and two tall, thin, rounded crests on its skull distinguished *Dilophosaurus*, the largest carnivorous dinosaur that lived in North America during the early Jurassic.

Its long back legs made it an agile runner, just as one would expect from a hunter dinosaur. Paleontologists aren't actually sure what *Dilophosaurus* ate, though. Some think that it fed on animals that were already dead, others think that it could pounce on prey even larger than itself, and others believe it was a "fisher," and therefore ate fish.

DISTINCTIVE FEATURES: a pair of parallel ridges on the skull

28

SAURUS

Its name means:
TWO-CRESTED LIZARD

WHERE IT LIVED:

North America

THE MYSTERY OF THE CRESTS

The function of *Dilophosaurus*'s two crests is still unknown. Their structure was too weak for them to be used in head-to-head battles with other dinosaurs because they would have been easily damaged. So the crests were likely shown off in mating displays, just like many birds do today. If this was the case, the crests could also have been brightly colored.

ITS WEIGHT:

880 lb. (400 kg)

ITS SIZE:

23 ft. (7 m) long

WHEN IT LIVED:

193 million years ago

| TRIASSIC | JURASSIC | CRETACEOUS |

AN X-RAY OF A DINOSAUR

In 2016, a group of paleontologists carefully examined a *Dilophosaurus* skeleton and found numerous traces of injuries and broken bones. Some of the vertebrae (bones that make up the spine), leg bones, and toe bones were damaged. So what happened? It is possible that all the damage was caused at the same time, perhaps by a fall during a fight. Since all the wounds had healed, the *Dilophosaurus* survived long after this event, definitely for months and maybe even for years.

CARNOT

Carnotaurus is one of the most well-known carnivorous dinosaurs to have lived in South America, and probably in the entire Southern Hemisphere, although only one skeleton has been found. The fossil, discovered in Argentina in 1984, is almost complete, with only the tail and lower legs missing. The rest of the skeleton, although slightly deformed from the weight of the **sediment** that preserved it, is in perfect condition. Thanks to this, we know that it was an adult and we have a very good idea of its body proportions. It was a large dinosaur with a straight, muscular neck and a short, high head. Its most distinctive features, however, were the two horns on its skull and its ridiculously short arms—even shorter than those of the more famous *Tyrannosaurus rex*.

Although the lower part of the hind legs is missing from the skeleton, the legs still suggest that this dinosaur was one of the fastest large carnivores. This hypothesis, or theory, also derives from the shape of the first tail vertebrae, to which the muscles that allow for movement of the legs—which must have been very well-developed—were attached.

Carnotaurus was most certainly a carnivore, but there are still doubts about what its prey might have been. Some scholars think it fed on medium-sized animals, while others believe it was also capable of catching large sauropods.

AURUS

Its name means:
MEAT-EATING BULL

WHERE IT LIVED:

South America

DISTINCTIVE FEATURES:
very short arms

ITS WEIGHT:

1.4 tons (1,400 kg)

ITS SIZE:

26–30 ft. (8–9 m) long

WHEN IT LIVED:

72–69 million years ago

TRIASSIC | JURASSIC | CRETACEOUS

UNIQUE HORNS

The skull, which is approximately 23.6 inches (60 cm) long, is proportionately shorter and stockier than that of other large carnivorous dinosaurs. Its most distinctive feature is the pair of cone-shaped horns above its eyes, which stick out sideways. *Carnotaurus* was the only bipedal carnivorous dinosaur to have horns like this. It is not clear what they were used for. One of the most probable hypotheses is that the horns were used in fights with other *Carnotaurus*, perhaps in the same way rams use their horns, withstanding the impact thanks to the muscular neck and very strong spine. They may have also been used during hunting, to kill small prey, or perhaps to show off in mating displays.

FOSSIL SKIN

Not only did the incredible state of preservation of the *Carnotaurus* fossil make it possible to create an almost complete skeleton, it also preserved traces of skin found in the rock underneath it. This made it possible to reconstruct different parts of its body: the head, jaw, neck, and thorax.

Its skin was made up of small scales measuring about 1/5 of an inch (0.5 cm). The skin also had several rows of **osteoderms**, which were stud-like bones, about 1.6–2 inches (4–5 cm) in diameter, that poked out of the skin and ran along the neck, back, and tail. Their function was probably to protect these areas, especially the sides, during clashes with their own kind or with other dinosaurs.

MICROR

Our knowledge about this dinosaur comes from more than 300 fossil specimens, which have allowed paleontologists to create a faithful reconstruction: It was small, it had hand and foot claws, both its arms and legs were covered with **wing feathers**, and it had sharp teeth, which it used to eat lizards, birds, and fish.

Its hunting technique, however, remains a mystery. The feathers on its arms were so long that they dragged on the ground as it ran, risking damage and preventing it from using its claws to grab prey.

DISTINCTIVE FEATURES: **two pairs of wings**

34

APTOR

Its name means:
SMALL THIEF

WHERE IT LIVED:

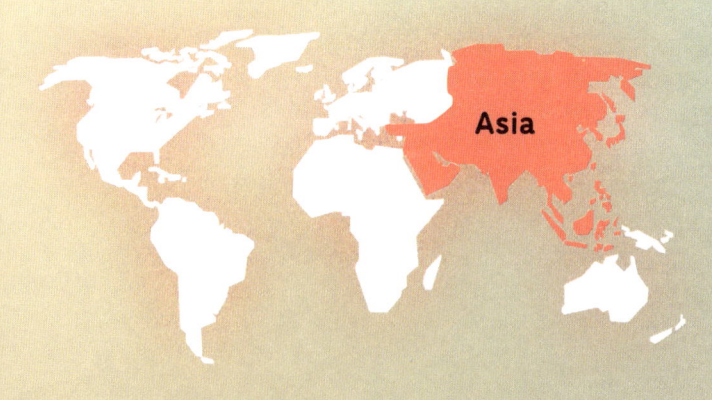

Asia

ITS WEIGHT:

2.2 lb. (1 kg)

ITS SIZE:

2.6–4 ft.
(80 cm–1.2 m) long

THE FIRST FLYING DINOSAUR

For a long time, scholars weren't sure if *Microraptor*'s four wings were used to slow down the fall when it launched itself from the branches of a tree or to glide from branch to branch. Almost all scholars now agree that this little dinosaur was capable of **flapping flight**, similar to today's birds.

WHEN IT LIVED:

120 million years ago

| TRIASSIC | JURASSIC | **CRETACEOUS** |

BLACK, BUT IRIDESCENT

Thanks to exceptionally well-preserved *Microraptor* fossils, in which the **quills** and body feathers are clearly visible, and to new ways of studying fossils, we also know a lot about its color. It was almost completely black with an iridescent sheen, and the two tail feathers were longer and shinier than the others in the tail fan. This coloring suggests that *Microraptor* was very active during the day, when its feathers could reflect the sunlight. The coloring may also have proved useful during mating displays.

35

CITIPAT

Citipati had a very long neck and a shorter tail than most other bipedal dinosaurs. The body was covered with fluffy feathers, while both the arms and tail had long feathers, which it used to keep its eggs warm. But this is not the only thing they have in common with today's birds. It had a crest on its head that was similar to that of a **cassowary** (a relative of the ostrich), and its skull, which was quite short, ended with a sturdy and completely toothless **beak**.

DISTINCTIVE FEATURES: **a large crest on its skull**

Its name means:
FUNERAL PYRE LORD

WHERE IT LIVED:

Asia

ITS WEIGHT:

165–187 lb.
(75–85 kg)

ITS SIZE:

10 ft. (3 m) long

BIG MAMA

In the 1990s, four *Citipati* specimens were found in nesting positions. They were on top of a cluster of eggs, with their legs spread out on each side of the nest and their arms completely covering it. This brooding behavior is typical of today's birds. The most famous of these specimens was nicknamed "Big Mama," due to its large size.

WHEN IT LIVED:

75–71 million years ago

| TRIASSIC | JURASSIC | CRETACEOUS |

PREY OR PREDATOR?

The skulls of two very young *Byronosauruses* were found inside a *Citipati* nest. They may have been so young they had not yet hatched from the eggs. Why were they there? Maybe they were prey that the *Citipati* brought to the nest to feed its chicks, or perhaps they were stealing from the nest. But there is also another hypothesis: an adult *Byronosaurus* may have laid its eggs in the *Citipati*'s nest, like today's cuckoos lay theirs in the nests of other birds.

GIGANOT

Giganotosaurus was the "*T. rex*" of the plains in present-day Patagonia and was the largest predator on the entire South American continent. It had three clawed fingers and curved, serrated teeth that were almost 8 inches (20 cm) long, allowing it to hunt dinosaurs much larger than itself, such as huge sauropods like the *Argentinosaurus*. Its bite caused severe injuries, as it effortlessly ripped off huge chunks of flesh and broke the bones of its prey.

DISTINCTIVE FEATURES:
short, wrinkled crests on its snout

...OSAURUS

Its name means:
GIANT SOUTHERN LIZARD

WHERE IT LIVED:

South America

ITS WEIGHT:

7.5 tons (6,800 kg)

ITS SIZE:

up to 46 ft. (14 m) long

WHEN IT LIVED:

99.6–97 million years ago

| TRIASSIC | JURASSIC | CRETACEOUS |

A DISPROPORTIONATE SKULL

Although an intact *Giganotosaurus* skull has never been found, the rest of the remains suggest that it had one of the largest. The skull could be up to 6 feet (1.8 m) long, which is almost ridiculously big compared to the body. However, its brain appears to be only the size and shape of a banana. A large area was dedicated to processing smells, and this probably meant that it could smell prey that were far away.

BIG AND FAST

Giganotosaurus had the longest legs of all **theropod** dinosaurs (such as *T. rex* or *Allosaurus*). Its skeletal structure, with the femur shorter than the tibia, allowed it to run quite fast. Some studies say that it could reach 30 miles (50 km) per hour. Combined with its lethal bite, this characteristic made *Giganotosaurus* a fearsome and active predator that preferred to hunt rather than settle for **carcasses**.

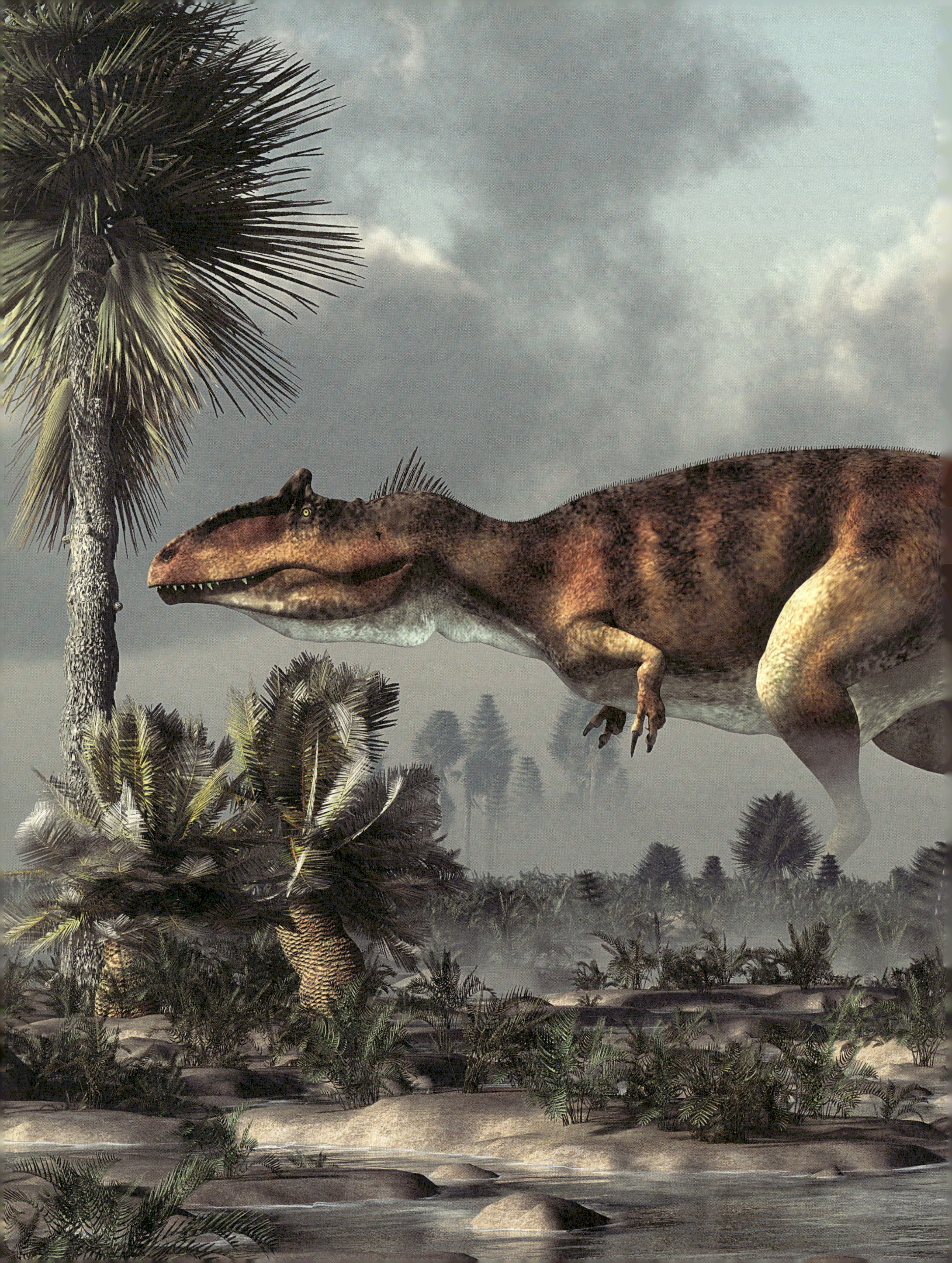

A Giganotosaurus *engaged in hunting*

VELOCIR

Velociraptor is one of the most famous dinosaurs, probably because it was the main character in a famous novel that was made into a movie series. In the movie it is a large, highly intelligent predator with scaly, greenish skin, taller than a man, that worked in groups to hunt prey. This was not an entirely accurate depiction. The real *Velociraptor* was a small, feathered dinosaur with a skull that could be up to 9.8 inches (25 cm) long. It basically looked like a large turkey with a long tail, a mouth full of sharp, serrated teeth, and numerous claws on its hands and feet. It also had a sickle claw on each foot, much longer than its other claws, which was probably used as a deadly weapon. The bone structure shows that this dinosaur was agile and fast, hence its name. Despite how Velociraptors have been shown as animals that hunt in packs, there is no evidence to suggest that they were social predators.

DISTINCTIVE FEATURES:
a long, curved claw on the second toe of each foot

APTOR

Its name means:
SPEEDY THIEF

WHERE IT LIVED:

Asia

ITS WEIGHT:

33–44 lb.
(15–20 kg)

ITS SIZE:

about 6.5 ft. (2 m) long

WHEN IT LIVED:

75–71 million years ago

| TRIASSIC | JURASSIC | CRETACEOUS |

WINGED THIEVES

The lizard-like image created by the movie industry was shattered in 2007, when scientists found evidence that *Velociraptor* was actually covered in feathers. A new fossil was unearthed in Mongolia, from the same rocks where all the other *Velociraptor* fossils have been found, and paleontologists found unquestionable signs on the forearm that it had feathers. It is therefore certain that its arms looked a lot like wings. Although their arms were very strong, *Velociraptor* were unable to fly because they were far too small to support their weight. Their arms were probably used to help them run faster and to keep their balance when they were standing over their prey.

Portrait of *Velociraptor mongoliensis* artist rendering

***Velociraptor mongoliensis* skull**

Velociraptor mongoliensis sickle claw

A LETHAL WEAPON

When *Velociraptor*'s distinctive sickle-shaped claw was first discovered, it was believed to be a perfect weapon for hunting—in fact, it was thought that the blows from its powerful hind legs were capable of ripping prey into pieces. However, the long, pointed claw wasn't at all sharp, so it is unlikely that this is what it was used for. *Velociraptor*'s hunting technique was probably to leap on its prey and hold it down with the sickle claws, devouring it while it was still alive.

A fossil of a *Velociraptor* locked in combat with a *Protoceratops*, with its claw in the *Protoceratops*'s throat, also suggests that it could use the claw to stab its prey and mortally wound it.

As they got older, or when they weren't in great shape, *Velociraptors* could also behave like **scavengers**—that is, feed on carrion, or flesh of dead animals.

This *Velociraptor* fossil shows details of the skeleton

45

Scientists found evidence that *Velociraptors* were actually covered in feathers. This artist's rendering of two alarmed *Velociraptors* shows what they might have looked like.

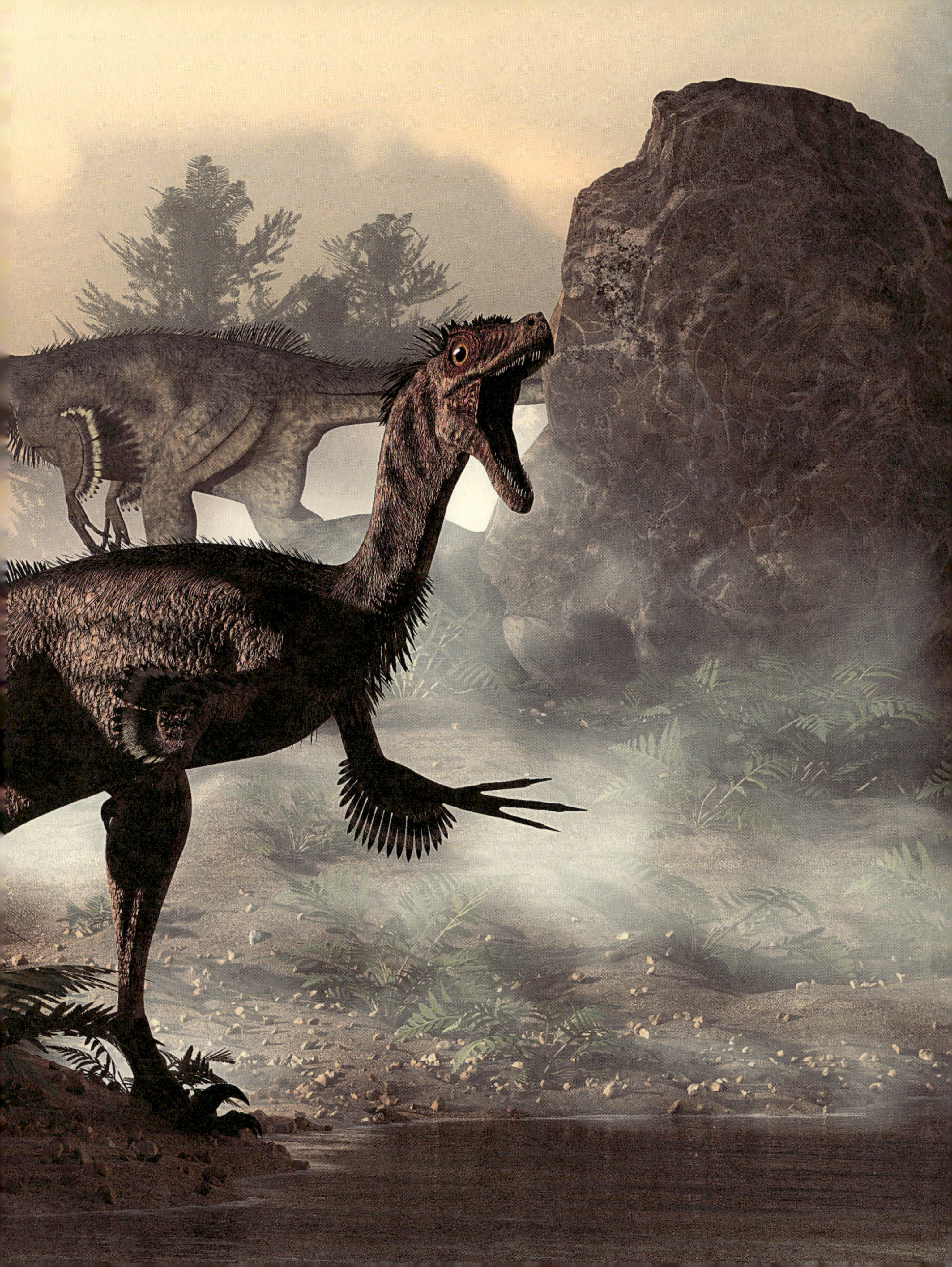

OVIRAPT

Oviraptor belongs to a group called oviraptorids, so named because it was the first dinosaur of this group to be discovered.

It was a feathered dinosaur, with long arms and a shortened skull, along with a beak that was similar to a parrot's.

Unfortunately, the only *Oviraptor* skull found is very damaged and missing some pieces.

O R

Its name means:
EGG THIEF

WHERE IT LIVED:

Asia

ITS WEIGHT:

73–88 lb.
(33–40 kg)

ITS SIZE:

approximately 5–6.5 ft.
(1.5–2 m) long

WHEN IT LIVED:

75–71 million years ago

TRIASSIC | JURASSIC | CRETACEOUS

DISTINCTIVE FEATURES:
a parrot-like beak

However, the appearance of some of its bones suggest that *Oviraptor* had a large, bony crest. This hypothesis became even more likely after the discovery of other members of the same group, such as *Citipati*, on which the crest is still clearly visible.

Its tail was also unusual. It was shorter than those of other similarly sized dinosaurs, and the final vertebrae were fused together. In birds, this structure, called a **pygostyle**, supports long tail feathers. This similarity suggested that *Oviraptor* had long feathers on its tail.

Its diet is still a bit of a mystery, but its beak was suitable for eating both small animals and seeds, plants, and eggs, which is why it is now considered omnivorous.

AN EGG THIEF?

This dinosaur's name was chosen in 1924 because the first specimen of *Oviraptor* was found on a cluster of eggs that were thought to be those of a *Protoceratops*, a small herbivorous, or plant-eating, dinosaur related to the much larger *Triceratops*. So what was the *Oviraptor* doing there?

The paleontologists' answer was very simple, although perhaps not quite correct—that it was stealing eggs for its lunch! But this was not the case. So what was the evidence that cleared *Oviraptor*'s name? In 1993, a chick was found inside an egg that was thought to be that of a *Protoceratops*, and...surprise! The chick was an *Oviraptor*! Also, over the next few years, several specimens of a dinosaur very similar to *Oviraptor* were found in brooding positions over a cluster of eggs. *Oviraptor* was therefore not guilty. Rather than stealing eggs from another dinosaur, it was hatching its own, just like almost all the dinosaurs belonging to its group.

GREEN-BLUE EGGS

Modern paleontological techniques, which make use of increasingly advanced instruments, have made it possible to figure out what was once impossible to know.

Oviraptorid eggs were found to contain two substances, **protoporphyrin** and **biliverdin**, which are in some eggshells of today's birds and are responsible for their coloring. This discovery has made it possible for scholars to know for sure that the eggs of this group of dinosaurs were a greenish-blue color.

TROODO

Troodon was a fairly small dinosaur, but it had a large brain for its size. Its brain was bigger than that of existing reptiles and very similar to a bird's. Its long hind legs made it quite fast, and its extremely flexible arms made hunting easier.

This dinosaur also had very large eyes that faced forward. This gave it perfect **binocular vision**, which meant it was able to accurately calculate distances when attacking its prey.

DISTINCTIVE FEATURES: very big eyes

Big eyes may have given *Troodon* a huge advantage over other predators in lower light conditions.

52

N

Its name means:
WOUNDING TOOTH

WHERE IT LIVED:

North America

ITS WEIGHT:

88 lb. (40 kg)

ITS SIZE:

6.5 ft. (2 m) long

WHEN IT LIVED:

77 million years ago

TRIASSIC | JURASSIC | CRETACEOUS

ITS DIET

Troodon probably ate any animal it could hunt. It often preyed on smaller species and on juveniles of larger species such as *Hadrosaurus* and *Edmontosaurus*. This hypothesis is also confirmed by the numerous *Troodon* bite marks on the bones of 95% of juvenile specimens of *Edmontosaurus*.

THE DISCOVERY OF A TOOTH

The first specimen of *Troodon* was a single tooth, which led to the discovery of this species. *Troodon*'s teeth were different from those of most other known animals. This made it difficult to describe the dinosaur. The teeth were sharp and curved like those of a carnivore, but they also had distinctive serrations similar to those of some herbivores. Since no other part of the skeleton had ever been seen, no one knew exactly what kind of dinosaur it was, or even if it was a dinosaur at all.

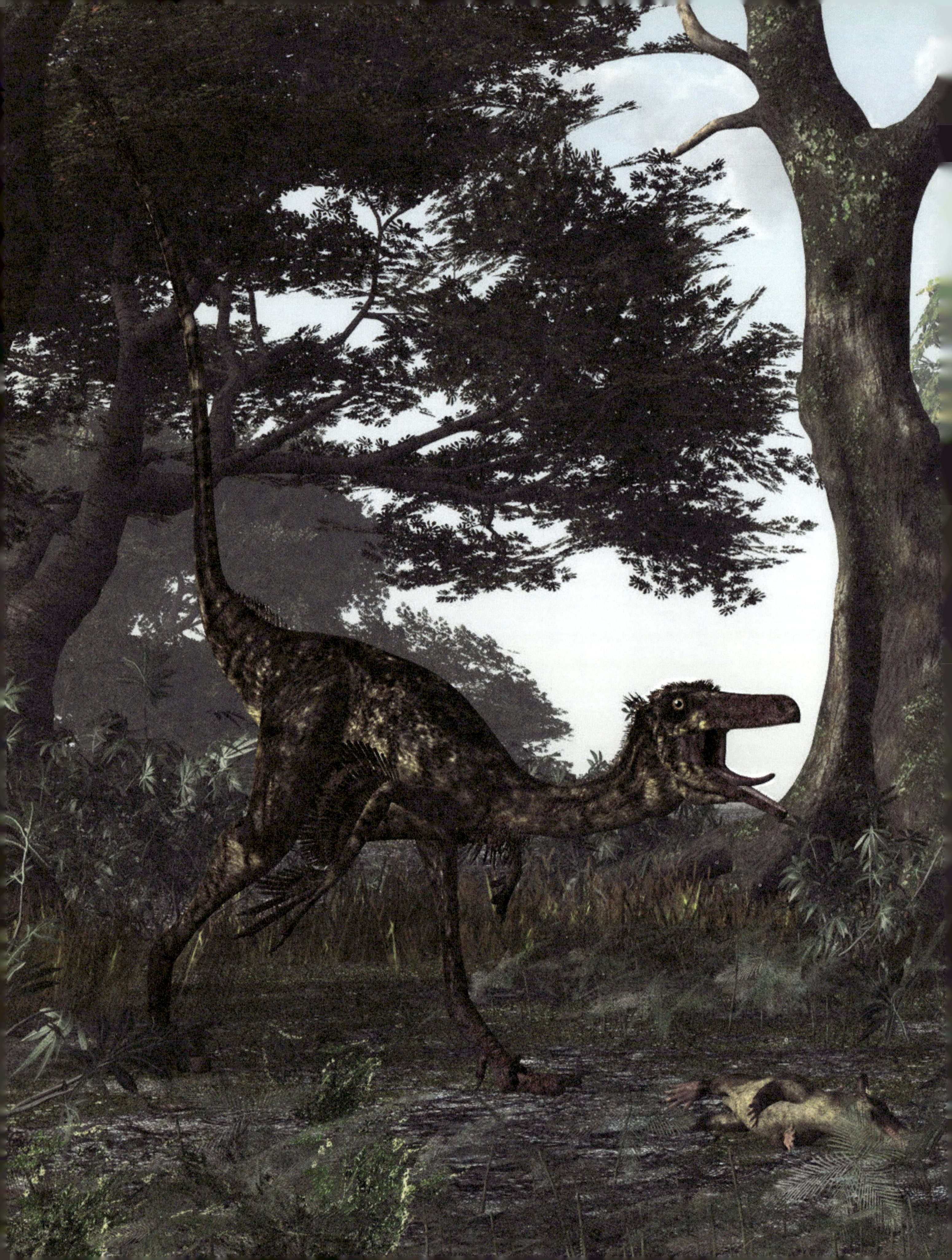

Two *Troodons* fighting over prey

ALLOSA

Allosaurus is perhaps the most famous of the many well-known carnivorous dinosaurs, at least of those that lived during the Jurassic period. It was discovered before the equally popular *T. rex*, and this is why for many years *Allosaurus* was what we imagined a large carnivorous dinosaur looked like. It undoubtably owes its fame to the numerous found skeletons of juvenile and adult specimens.

The large number of fossil discoveries has made it possible for us to know how this dinosaur developed and behaved. It lived for at least 28 years and became an adult between the ages of 13 and 19. Its body proportions changed slightly as it grew. Juvenile specimens had longer hind legs than adults compared to the size of the rest of the body. This suggests that juveniles were more agile and faster, and therefore more suited to active hunting and pursuits, while adults would stalk their prey.

DISTINCTIVE FEATURES: small ridges above its eyes

URUS

Its name means:
DIFFERENT LIZARD

WHERE IT LIVED:

North America
Europe
Africa

ITS WEIGHT:

1.4–2 tons
(1,400–1,800 kg)

ITS SIZE:

about 33 ft. (10 m) long

WHEN IT LIVED:

155–145 million years ago

TRIASSIC | JURASSIC | CRETACEOUS

PACK LIFE?

For a long time, it was believed that *Allosauruses* lived in packs, due to many skeletons being found in the same place. However, some findings suggest that it was quite the opposite. Various skeletons show signs of fighting between species. Although encounters between *Allosauruses* were frequent, they were certainly not friendly.

HUNTING

Like most carnivorous dinosaurs, *Allosaurus*'s most lethal weapons were its claws and, above all, its teeth. Those teeth were pointed, serrated, and short, which left scholars uncertain for a long time about how the teeth were used during hunting. Today, it is thought that *Allosaurus* used its entire head to kill its prey with a combination of blunt force and puncture wounds. Its extremely muscular neck helped the skull to strike the prey, while the *Allosaurus* kept its mouth wide open so its teeth could tear off large pieces of meat.

This reconstructed skeleton that can be admired at a museum also serves to compare the size of the dinosaur with humans

Its arms were very powerful, allowing it to hold down its victims with its fearsome curved claws, which were about 7 inches (18 cm) long.

Thanks to these powerful weapons, an *Allosaurus* could conquer prey much bigger than itself, such as *Diplodocus*. Once it had killed its prey, the *Allosaurus* fed on it just like large birds of prey do today: it climbed onto the prey's body, holding it down with its hind legs, and, thanks to the flexibility and strength of its neck, it would bite into the carcass and rip it apart.

However, it didn't always come out of these encounters unharmed. Scientists discovered one of its vertebrae with a clearly visible wound caused by the spiny tail of a *Stegosaurus*.

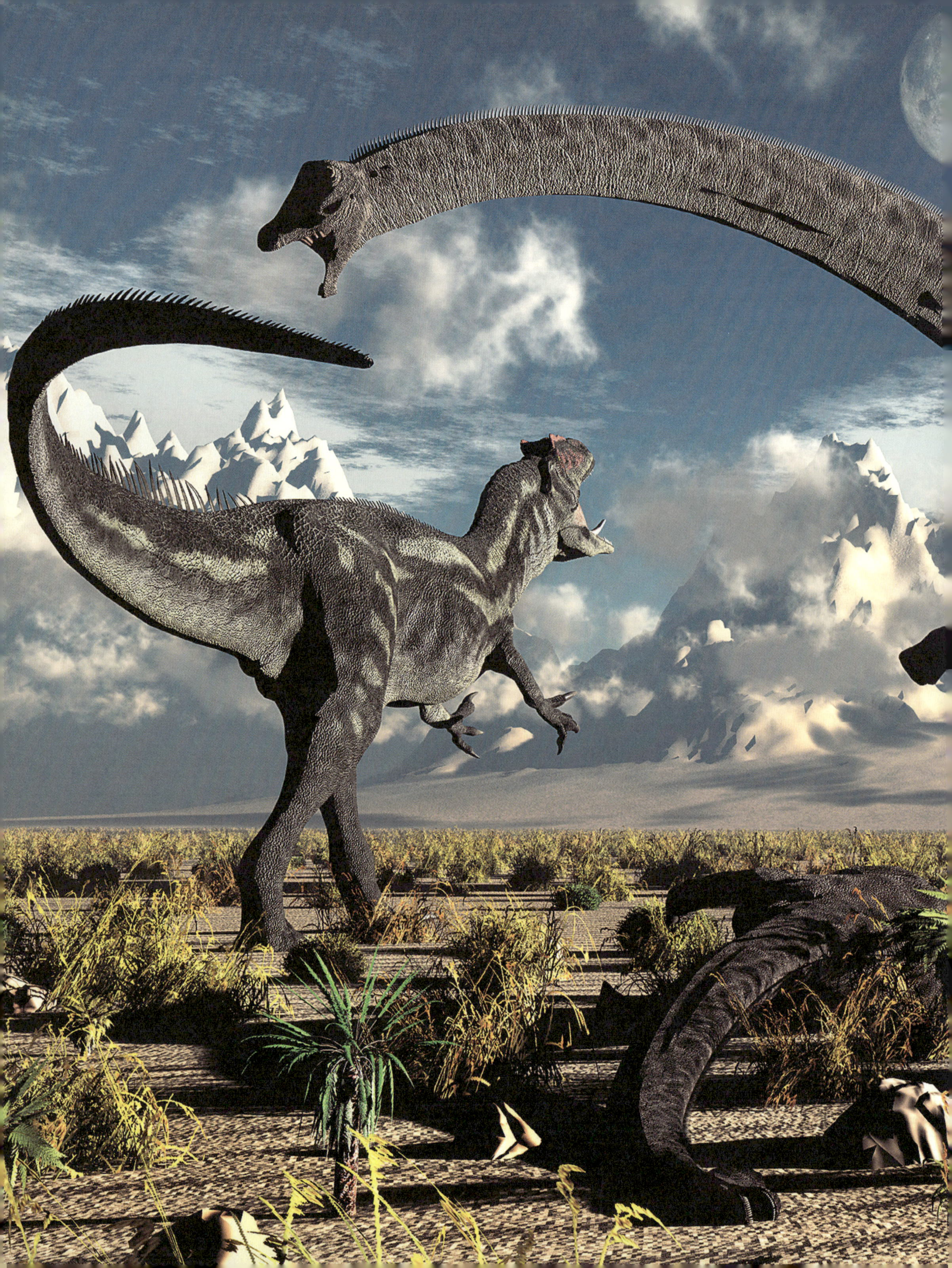

A large *Diplodocus* tries to defend itself against a pair of *Allosauruses,* which have already attacked and killed a young *Diplodocus*

CERATO

Ceratosaurus fossils are quite rare, but they are immediately recognizable because this large carnivorous dinosaur had a distinctive nasal **horn** and two other horny bumps over both eyes. Unlike most carnivorous dinosaurs, it had a row of small bony plates along its back, called **osteoderms**, which acted as protective armor.

This dinosaur had strong jaws with very long, blade-like teeth. Its arms were short, but they could still be used to grab and hold down prey.

DISTINCTIVE FEATURES: two crests that protected its eyes

SAURUS

Its name means:
HORNED LIZARD

WHERE IT LIVED:

North America
Europe

ITS WEIGHT:

1,100 lb. (500 kg)

ITS SIZE:

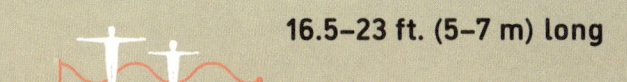

16.5–23 ft. (5–7 m) long

WHEN IT LIVED:

157–152 million years ago

| TRIASSIC | JURASSIC | CRETACEOUS |

RIVAL DINOSAURS?

Ceratosaurus fossils are often found with those of other large carnivores, including the famous *Allosaurus*. Paleontologists wonder how two large predators could live together in the same environment and whether they competed with each other for food. Obviously, there is no way to know for certain, so only hypotheses can be made. Perhaps they had different hunting strategies: *Ceratosaurus* was more skilled at hunting aquatic prey, such as fish, crocodiles, and turtles, while *Allosaurus* preferred large herbivorous dinosaurs.

WEAPON OR DECORATION?

The nasal horn is one of *Ceratosaurus*'s most well-known features, but what was it used for? It was once believed to be a weapon for both attacking and defending itself, but the horn might have been used during combat with rival male *Ceratosauruses* over access to females. Some scholars think that the horn was just used in mating displays, like a peacock's tail fan. If this was the case, it may also have been very colorful.

ICHTHYOV

Ichthyovenator was a spinosaurid dinosaur and an Asian relative of the later and larger *Spinosaurus*. The two share several characteristics, such as a dorsal **sail**, sturdy arms with sharp claws on the toes and fingers, and a long, thin snout—at least this is what is believed, since an *Ichthyovenator* skull has never been found. Its snout and cone-shaped teeth, with no sharp edges or serrations, were perfect for hunting wet and slippery prey such as fish or other aquatic animals, and this is where its name comes from.

DISTINCTIVE FEATURES: a sail split in two

Ichthyovenator lived alongside sauropods such as *Tangvayosaurus*

ENATOR

Its name means:
FISH HUNTER

WHERE IT LIVED:

Asia

ITS WEIGHT:

2.4 tons (2,200 kg)

ITS SIZE:

27 ft. (8.5 m) long

WHEN IT LIVED:

125–113 million years ago

TRIASSIC | JURASSIC | CRETACEOUS

A SAIL SPLIT IN TWO

Ichthyovenator's dorsal sail was just over 1.5 feet (0.5 m) high and an unusual shape that made it stand out from that of other spinosaur. The sail was wavy, dipping downward at the hips and the beginning of the tail, and ending about halfway along the tail. The sail's use has long been debated, but today it is widely believed to have been used in mating displays.

AQUATIC ADAPTATIONS

If we consider *Ichthyovenator*'s ability to hunt aquatic animals, we might wonder how much of its life was spent near rivers or other bodies of water. Like other spinosaurs, *Ichthyovenator* had several adaptations that made it especially suited to aquatic environments, such as bones heavier than those of other dinosaurs and a tail similar to modern-day crocodilians, that make swimming easier.

SPINOSA

The first *Spinosaurus* fossils were unearthed from the sand in the Egyptian desert in 1912. They were described three years later by the German paleontologist Ernst Stromer, who named the dinosaur after the huge spines on its dorsal, or the back, vertebrae. This dinosaur was clearly different from other large predators that had been found, but Stromer could never have imagined just how much! In addition to the vertebrae, other remains were found, including several teeth, some ribs, and a fragment of the jaw. Unfortunately, this skeleton was completely destroyed in the bombing of Munich during the night of April 24–25, 1944, when the Bavarian State Collection of Paleontology and Geology, where it was exhibited, was seriously damaged. The *Spinosaurus* that had emerged from the sand 32 years earlier was reduced to ashes, although detailed descriptions and drawings survived. Over the next few years, new fossils were found throughout North Africa, but only a few teeth and some small bone fragments.

DISTINCTIVE FEATURES: a tall sail on the back and a tail fin

URUS

Its name means:
SPINE LIZARD

WHERE IT LIVED:

Africa

ITS WEIGHT:

7 tons
(6,300 kg)

ITS SIZE:

49 ft. (15 m) long

WHEN IT LIVED:

100–93 million years ago

TRIASSIC	JURASSIC	CRETACEOUS

In the 1970s, a snout about 3 feet (1 m) long was unearthed, but it was only between 2008 and 2020 that *Spinosaurus*'s true appearance was revealed to the world. Numerous excavations in the Moroccan desert, carried out by an international team of paleontologists, brought to light the most complete *Spinosaurus* skeleton yet.

This largest carnivorous dinosaur ever known was **quadrupedal** and perfectly adapted to aquatic life. It had a crocodile-like snout with pressure sensors to detect prey in murky water, a mouth filled with teeth that were conical (shaped like cones) and perfect for catching fish, sturdy arms with clawed fingers for grabbing slippery prey, webbed hind feet, and a **fin**-like tail that made it an excellent swimmer, unlike any other dinosaur.

67

This new information made it possible to solve a problem known as **Stromer's Riddle**. Usually, there were more herbivores than carnivores, but it seemed to have been the opposite in the North African desert. Also, the presence of two large predators like *Spinosaurus* and *Carcharodontosaurus* (a carnivore as large as a *T. rex*) was really difficult to explain. However, if *Spinosaurus* was mainly an aquatic hunter, and *Carcharodontosaurus* a land hunter, it all made sense. Neither of them would have invaded the territory of the other or eaten its prey.

AN UNUSUAL TAIL

Spinosaurus's most amazing feature was without a doubt its tail. The vertebrae are completely different from those of any other dinosaur tail found so far. Each vertebra had a spine on top, about 24 inches (60 cm) long, making the tail very similar to the fin-like tail of a crested newt, except the tail was over 3 feet (1 m) high.

Spinosaurus was the first dinosaur to have a real fin, making it perfect for swimming in the waters of the vast river system that occupied much of North Africa in the Cretaceous.

THE SAIL

Spinosaurus had the largest sail of all the spinosaurs, growing to a maximum height of over 6.5 feet (2 m). Paleontologists have been studying its function since it was discovered, hypothesizing that it could have been used to regulate the dinosaur's body temperature or even for storing fat. Recent studies have confirmed that it was a thin sail but also have ruled out that it was used for thermoregulation. Today, *Spinosaurus*'s sail is thought to have been used for identifying others of the species, mating displays, or to appear larger in order to intimidate those invading its fishing territory.

Spinosaurus's tooth

69

BARYON

DISTINCTIVE FEATURES: a long, heavy claw on each hand

Its name means:
HEAVY CLAW

WHERE IT LIVED:

Europe

ITS WEIGHT:

1.2–1.7 tons
(1,200–1,700 kg)

ITS SIZE:

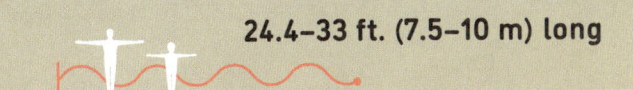

24.4–33 ft. (7.5–10 m) long

WHEN IT LIVED:

130–125 million years ago

TRIASSIC | JURASSIC | CRETACEOUS

Baryonyx is a genus of spinosaurid dinosaur whose fossils were found for the first time in England in 1983 and later on the Iberian Peninsula. The British specimen of this carnivorous dinosaur immediately became a star because it was the largest and most complete skeleton found in the United Kingdom for decades.

The features that made *Baryonyx* unique at that time were its thin, tapered snout, estimated to be just under 3 feet (1 m) long, strong arms, and powerful hands with three fingers with large claws. There was also a small triangular crest on the skull.

Like *Spinosaurus*, *Baryonyx*'s jaw was much narrower at the front, and the tip of the snout expanded to the sides in the shape of a rosette. However, unlike its larger relative, the upper set of teeth was considerably different to the lower one: the curved, finely serrated conical teeth in the **maxilla**, or upper jaw, were much larger and more spaced out than those in the **mandible**, or lower jaw. This, combined with the length and distinctive structure of the skull, suggests that *Baryonyx* was a **piscovore**, or fish eater.

This theory was proved when the semi-digested scales and teeth of a fish were found in its skeleton. However, there were also the remains of a juvenile *Iguanodon*, leading some scholars to believe that it may also have fed on carrion.

A HEAVY CLAW

Paleontologists decided to name this dinosaur after the large claw that was found with the skeleton. The claw was curved, pointed, and 12 inches (31 cm) long. But there was a problem: the claw had been separated from the rest of the skeleton, so it was not clear whether it belonged to the hands or feet. Furthermore, at first it was mistakenly thought to be similar to a *Velociraptor*'s claw. Later studies confirmed that it was from the first finger of the hand. So what was it used for? Probably for grabbing fish in the water, holding down larger ones, and ripping carrion apart.

BIPED OR QUADRUPED?

The debate on how spinosaurs moved has always been very heated. They are very long dinosaurs with extremely strong arms. From the moment *Baryonyx* was discovered, some scholars guessed that it could walk on all four limbs. To support this theory, in 2014 it was proven that *Spinosaurus* had a forward-leaning center of gravity, making it necessary for it to support its weight with its arms. However, there is another spinosaur, *Suchomimus*, a closer relation of *Baryonyx*, whose hind legs were so long that quadrupedal walking would have been impossible, making it unlikely that *Baryonyx* would have been able to, either.

AUSTROR

Austroraptor is the largest dromaeosaur ever discovered in South America, and it has many characteristics that make it unique among its group. Its arms were short compared to those of other dromaeosaurids, and its skull was narrow and long, indicating that the jaw muscles were underdeveloped and therefore had a weaker bite force. Finally, unlike other dromaeosaurs, its teeth were not serrated and laterally flattened, much like human teeth are, but instead were conical and suited for holding slippery prey, not good for tearing flesh.

It is therefore possible that *Austroraptor* was a predator of just one type of prey. The underdeveloped arms suggest that this dinosaur probably didn't hunt large prey but was better suited to catching small animals, despite its large size. The *Austroraptor* relied on its speed to chase prey and attack them from behind, stabbing them with the huge claws on its feet. The *Austroraptor* perhaps also used its claws to catch fish in shallow water, where it could then pick them up with its teeth and carry them ashore, where it would use its claws again to rip them up into small pieces that were easier to swallow.

The *Austroraptor* could also have been a scavenger, using its size to chase smaller hunters away from their prey, while using its speed to escape larger ones.

DISTINCTIVE FEATURES: short arms

APTOR

Its name means:
SOUTHERN THIEF

WHERE IT LIVED:

South America

ITS WEIGHT:

up to 660 lb. (300 kg)

ITS SIZE:

16.5 ft. (5 m) long

WHEN IT LIVED:

70 million years ago

TRIASSIC | JURASSIC | CRETACEOUS

THE GIANTS OF THE FAMILY

For a long time, paleontologists thought that dromaeosaurs were not very big. That was until 1993, when *Utahraptor* was presented to the world. It was a large, 23-foot-long (7 m) dromaeosaur, weighing over half a ton, and it had a 9.5-inch-long (24 cm) sickle claw, which would have been much longer when the animal was alive, and a layer of keratin, the same substance our nails are made of, covered the claw.

The *Utahraptor* was found a few years later than *Austroraptor*, which is 16.5 feet (5 m) long, and added another giant to the group.

Its arms were shorter than those of its smaller relatives and resembled those of *Allosaurus*. This confirms something that has been observed in some carnivorous dinosaurs: the larger the body, the shorter the arms.

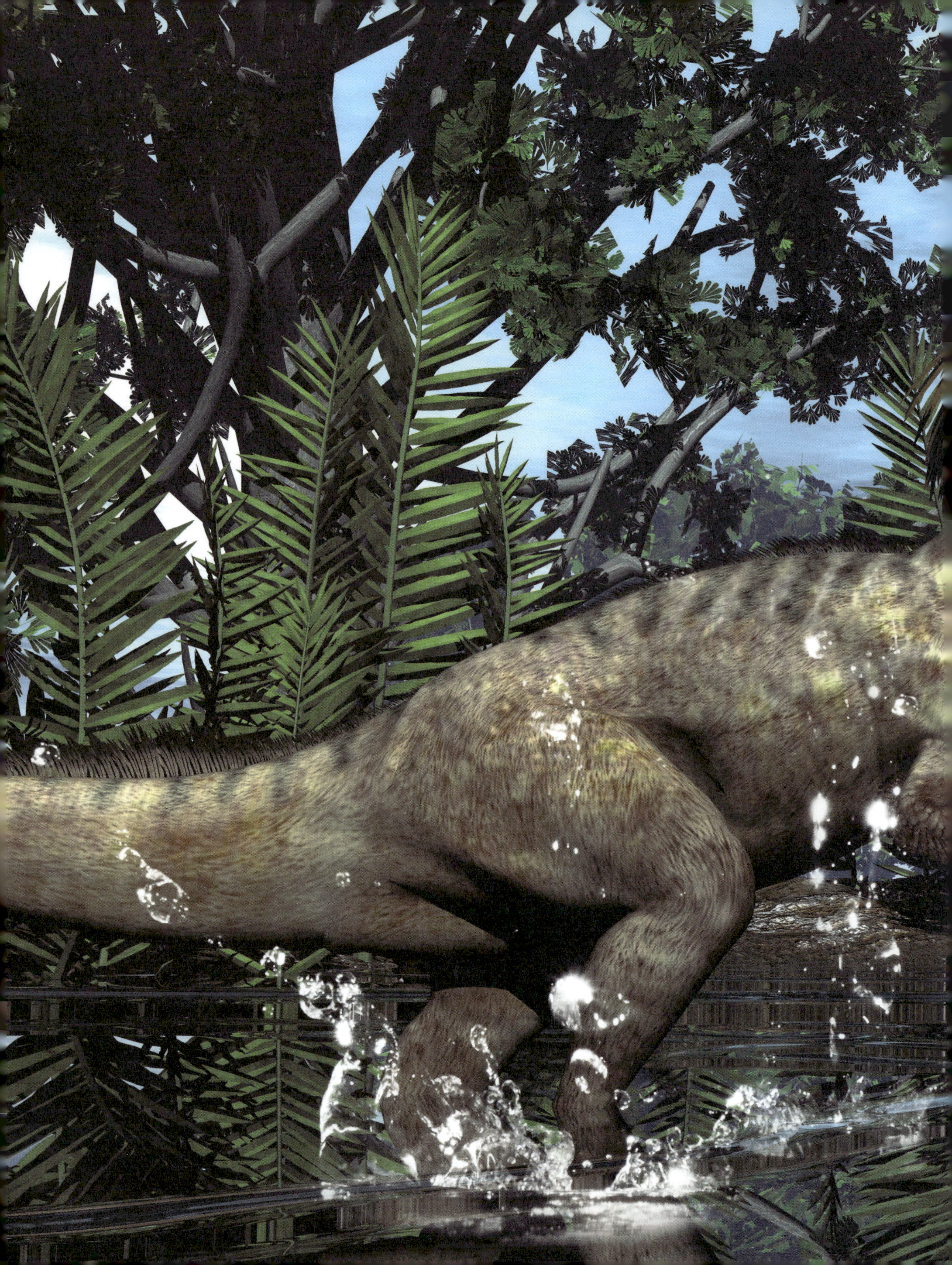

An *Austroraptor* is fishing. Both the dinosaur and fish existed at the same time, in the late Cretaceous period

ACROCANT

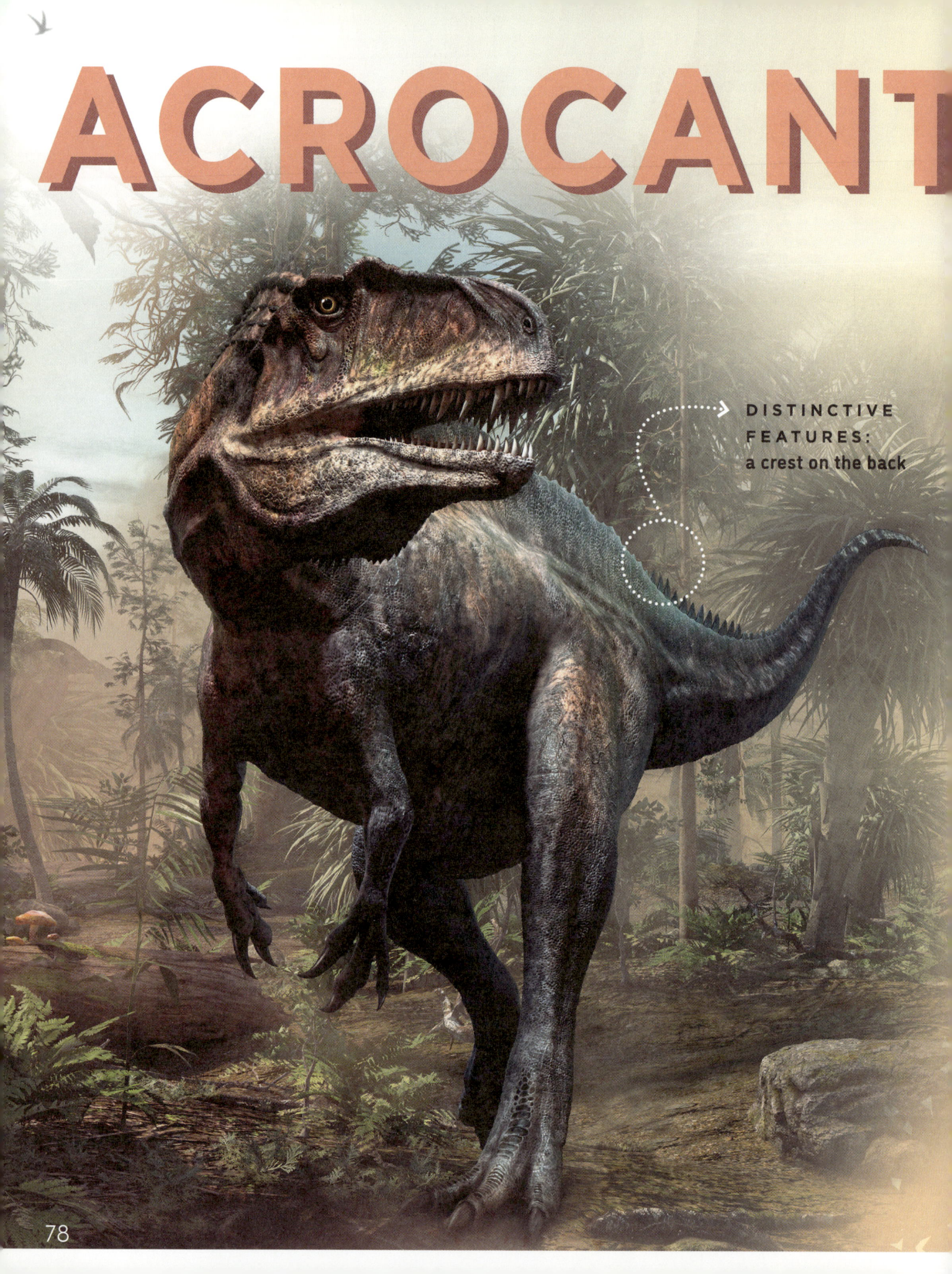

DISTINCTIVE FEATURES: a crest on the back

HOSAURUS

Its name means: HIGH-SPINED LIZARD

WHERE IT LIVED:

North America

ITS WEIGHT:

6.8 tons (6,200 kg)

ITS SIZE:

37.7 ft. (11.5 m) long

WHEN IT LIVED:

125–100 million years ago

TRIASSIC | JURASSIC | CRETACEOUS

Acrocanthosaurus was one of the largest carnivorous dinosaurs. Its skull alone was nearly 4.5 feet (1.3 m) in length, which is truly massive. There were two ridges along the entire length of its snout, from the nose to above the eyes, and the jaw had thirty-eight curved teeth that were close together.

But *Acrocanthosaurus*'s most distinctive feature was the vertebrae of the neck, back, and upper tail. The shape and size of these bones suggest that the dinosaur had an enormous crest on its back. Its function is not clear. It may have been used to store fat, or was a way to control body temperature; or maybe it was a kind of "ornament," or decoration, used to recognize others of its species.

The structure of the hind legs suggests that *Acrocanthosaurus* was not a very fast runner. Despite this, it is believed to have been a hunter, because of its large size. Its main weapon was its mouth, which it used to attack prey before grabbing it and holding it down with its arms. *Acrocanthosaurus* coexisted with numerous other dinosaurs and was the largest predator in its habitat. Its prey included sauropods, such as juvenile specimens of the gigantic *Sauroposeidon*, a long-necked dinosaur that was a relative of the better-known *Brachiosaurus*.

INSIDE THE HEAD OF A DINOSAUR

In 2005, paleontologists performed a **CT scan** (a medical exam used like an x-ray to see inside the body) on a *Acrocanthosaurus* skull. They wanted to see what it looked like inside and to try to econstruct the size and shape of its brain. This is how they discovered that its brain was S-shaped, very similar to those of today's crocodiles, and that it had a very large area dedicated to scent, called the olfactory bulb.

WAS ACROCANTHOSAURUS A DANCER?

In 2016, a strange set of long footprints were found in the United States. At first, paleontologists didn't know what they were, but after analyzing them, they discovered marks left by claws.

They were the footprints of large carnivorous dinosaurs, although they were a very unusual shape, as if the feet that left them had been scraping the ground. The tracks were very similar to those produced by birds as they "scrape" the ground with their claws during mating rituals. This could be the first fossil evidence of mating dances also being performed by the huge reptiles of the past. But which dinosaur left these footprints? Given the place they were found, their size, and the period they are from—the Cretaceous—it could very well have been an *Acrocanthosaurus*.

Reconstruction of an *Acrocanthosaurus* footprint

GALLIMI

Gallimimus was found in Mongolia. Like the American *Struthiomimus*, it is part of the large group of dinosaurs that paleontologists call ornithomimosaurs, which are similar to large birds like the ostrich or emu. However, unlike the emu, *Gallimimus* had a long tail for maintaining balance while running, long arms, and three fingers with straight and not very sharp claws. The structure of the hind legs shows that this dinosaur was a skilled runner, perhaps the fastest of its time. This ability was certainly useful for escaping possible predators, which it could easily detect thanks to the large eyes on the sides of its head.

DISTINCTIVE FEATURES: long, well-built arms

MUS

Its name means:
CHICKEN MIMIC

WHERE IT LIVED:

Asia

A LONER OR PART OF A GROUP?

Many fossils of *Gallimimus* juveniles and adults have been found, but never together. This could suggest that they lived alone. However, three adults and eleven juvenile ornithomimosaurs belonging to a similar species were found together, which could be evidence that *Gallimimus* also lived in groups.

ITS WEIGHT:

990–1,100 lb. (450–500 kg)

ITS SIZE:

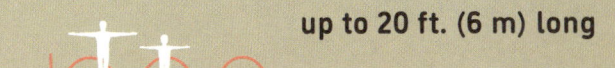

up to 20 ft. (6 m) long

WHEN IT LIVED:

72–68 million years ago

| TRIASSIC | JURASSIC | CRETACEOUS |

A LITTLE-KNOWN DIET

The structure of *Gallimimus*'s skull, with its toothless beak similar to a duck's bill, has made it difficult to figure out exactly what this dinosaur ate. It most likely ate land animals such as small reptiles or insects. It likely also ate plants and mollusks, which it would find near the freshwater pools that were probably its natural habitat. This means that *Gallimimus* was an omnivorous dinosaur.

TYRANNO

Tyrannosaurus is definitely the world's most famous dinosaur. It owes its fame to literature and films, in which it often plays the leading role, although almost always as the "bad guy." This dinosaur is so well known that most people even know its full scientific name, *Tyrannosaurus rex*, although it is often called by its more friendly nickname, *T. rex*.

The first skeleton was found in the early 20th century, and since then about fifty more have been unearthed, some of them almost complete. These include "Stan" (1987), which was sold in 2020 for $31.8 million, "Sue" (1990), who at 28 years old appears to be the oldest found so far, and "Scotty" (1991), the largest ever found, with an estimated length of almost 46 feet (14 m).

Tyrannosaurus was bipedal, with long, powerful hind legs, very short but muscular arms, and only two fingers on each hand.

> **DISTINCTIVE FEATURES:** the most powerful bite of all land animals

SAURUS

Its name means:
TYRANT LIZARD

WHERE IT LIVED:

North America

ITS WEIGHT:

over 9 tons (8,000 kg)

ITS SIZE:

41–46 ft. (12.5–14 m) long

WHEN IT LIVED:

70–66 million years ago

| TRIASSIC | JURASSIC | CRETACEOUS |

It is not entirely clear what it used its arms for, but it could have been to help it get back on its feet. Its skull could be almost 5 feet (1.5 m) long, and its mouth was armed with almost sixty teeth, which could be up to 12 inches (30 cm) long. It had the most powerful bite of all land animals—so powerful it would have been able to crush a car. There are fossils of dinosaurs related to *Tyrannosaurus*, such as *Yutyrannus*, that show evidence of feathers, suggesting that some parts of *T. rex*'s body may also have been feathered, although no proof of this has been found.

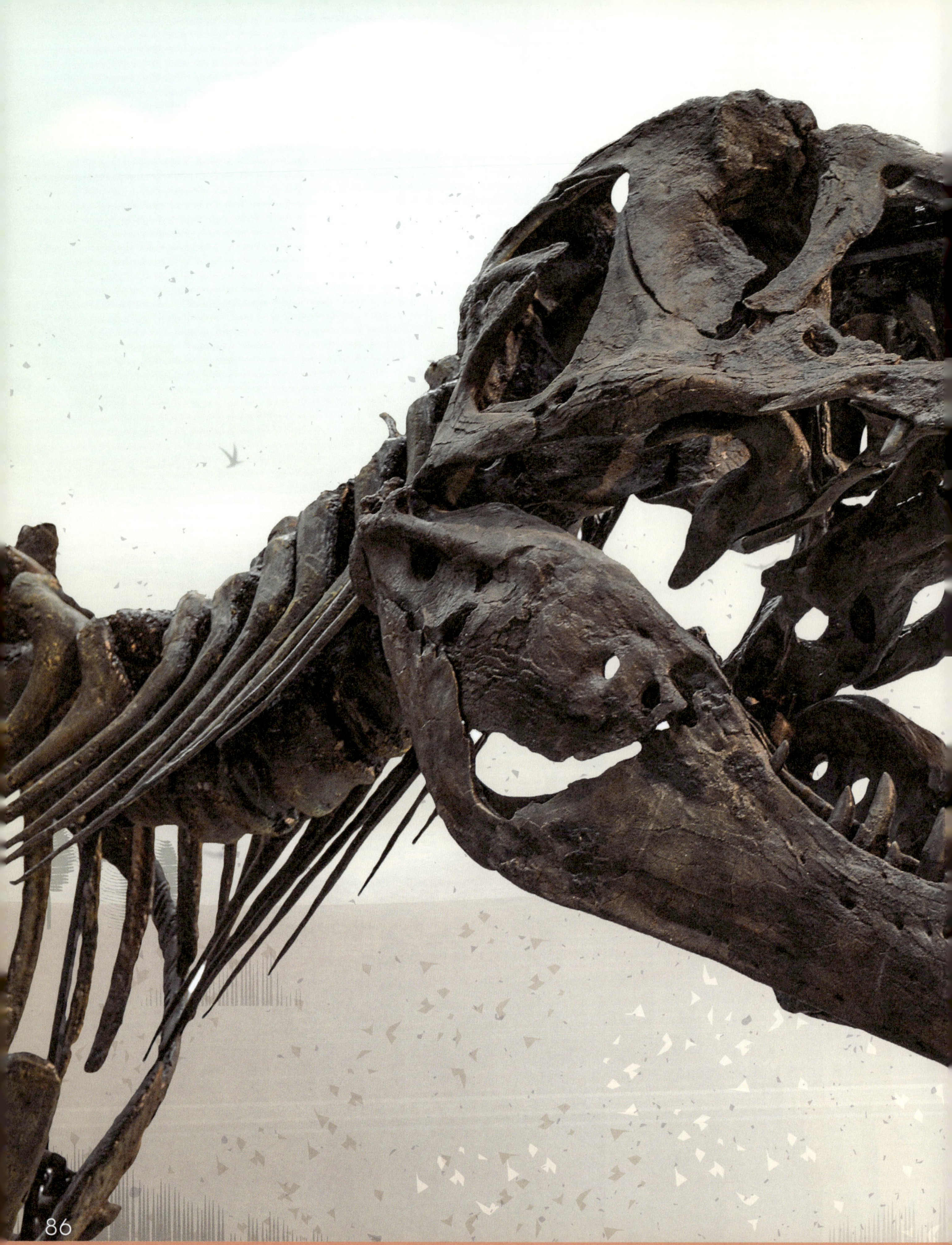

T. rex's claw

A SCARY MOM

In 2016, a particular bone tissue called medullary bone was found in a 68-million-year-old *T. rex* femur. The researcher could not believe her eyes, since medullary bone is only found today in female birds before and during egg-laying, and it stores calcium for eggshell production. There was only one explanation: the specimen had died while the eggs were forming in its abdomen, and the researcher was therefore looking at the bone of a *Tyrannosaurus* "mom."

PREDATOR OR SCAVENGER?

There are basically two hypotheses on the diet of *T. rex*: some believe it was a skilled hunter and others believe it was a **scavenger** and ate carrion. The reason for this uncertainty came from the results of studies on its ability to run and on its brain. The structure of its hind legs means that it could not have been a fast runner, and the part of the brain regulating the sense of smell was especially well developed, which meant it could detect a carcass over a long distance. On the other hand, while not a sprinter, it was probably faster than any of its potential prey, such as *Triceratops* and hadrosaurs ("duck-billed" dinosaurs). *Tyrannosaurus* was also gifted with incredibly sharp eyesight thanks to the size of its eyes and their placement in the skull, even sharper than that of a hawk, which was ideal for a predator.

In 2014, a series of footprints found in Canada could have belonged to a group of tyrannosaurs moving together, and this could be evidence of them hunting in packs. *Tyrannosaurus* was probably an opportunistic carnivore, which means that although it hunted fresh meat, it also took opportunities to eat carcasses and carrion. It also seems that it was a **cannibal**: in 2010, marks found on the foot bones of a *T. rex* appeared to be made by teeth of another *Tyrannosaurus*. Since it would have been very difficult to bite feet during combat, the specimen was probably already dead when it was eaten.

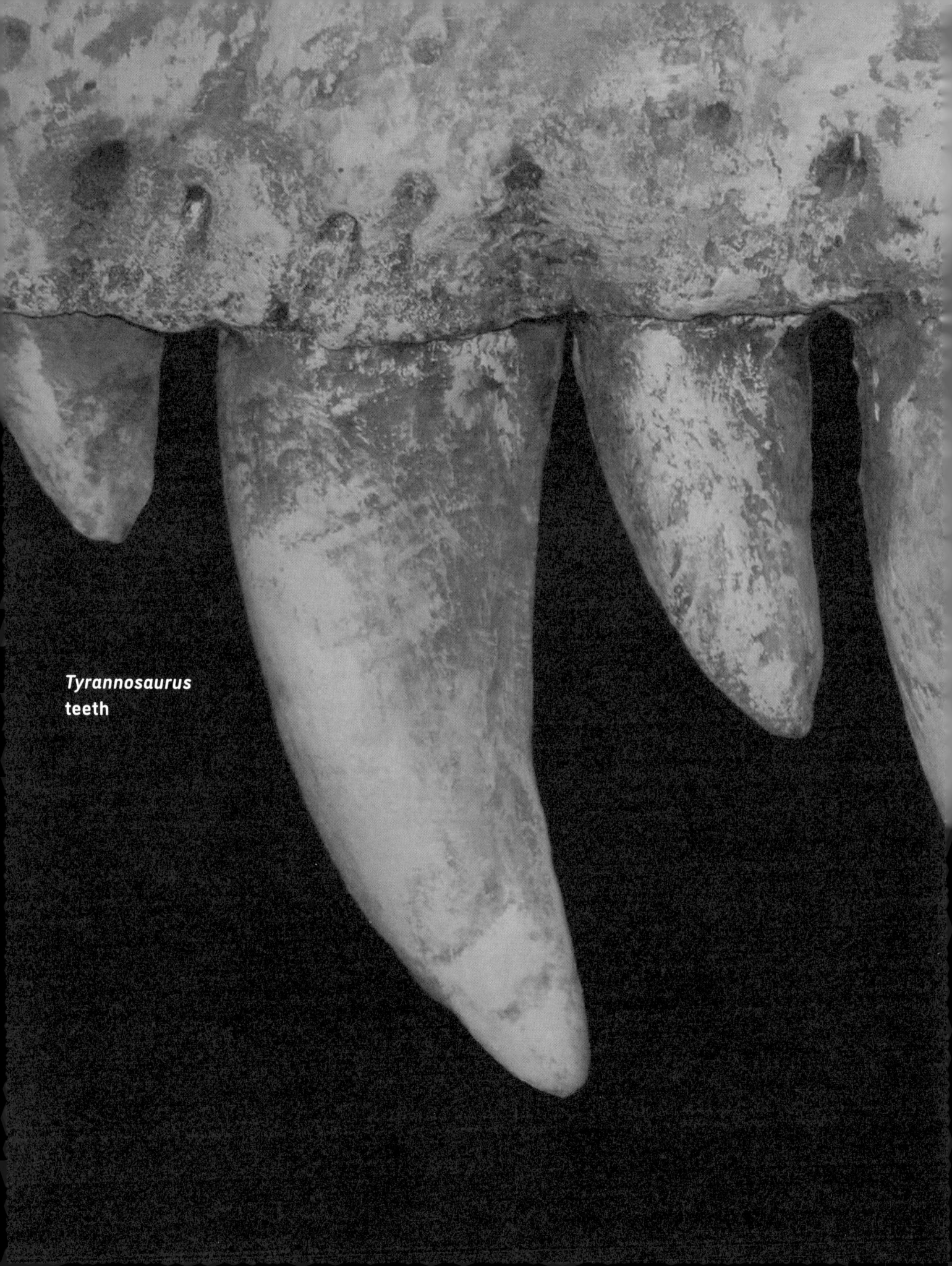

Tyrannosaurus teeth

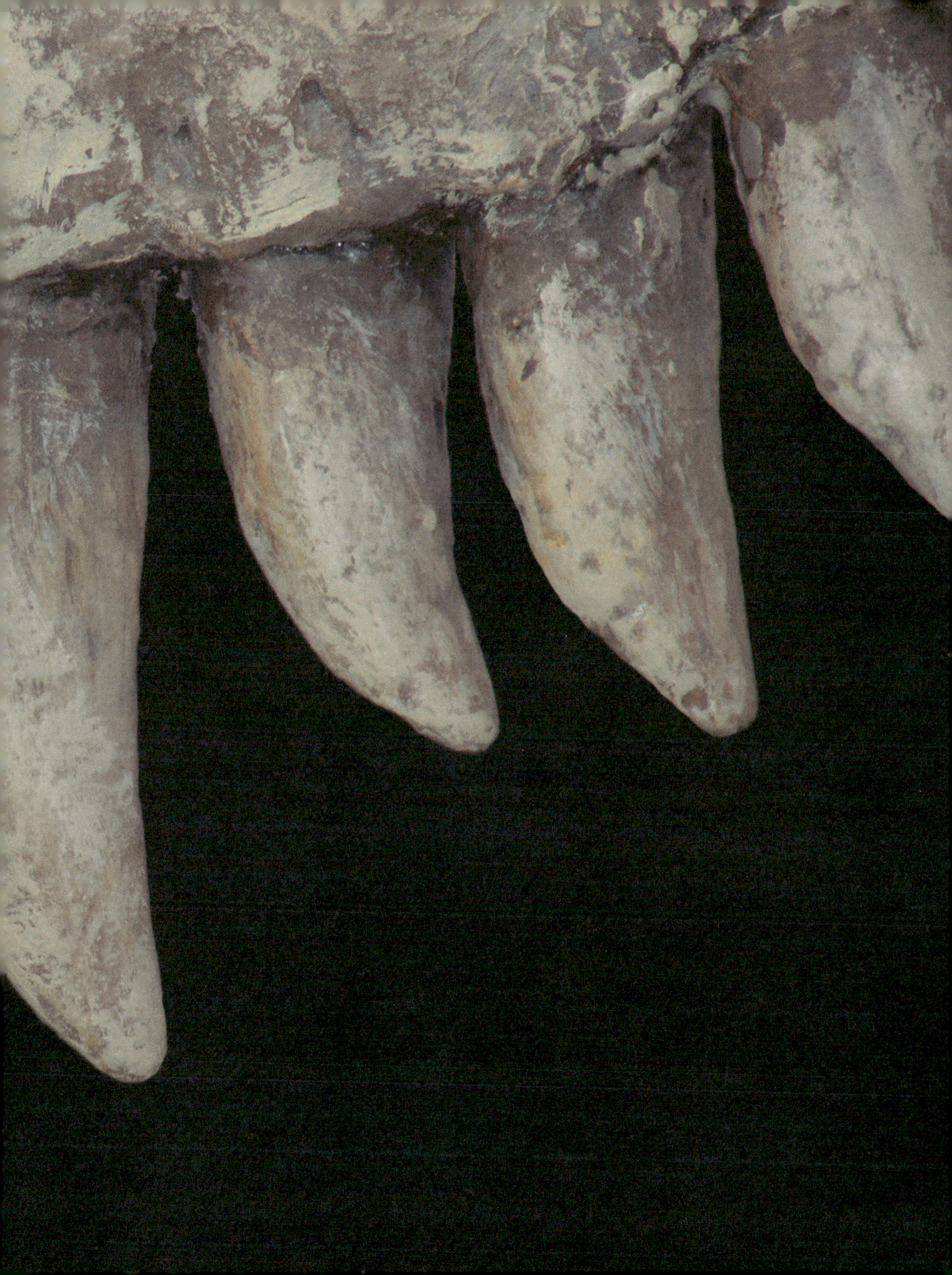

ARCHAEO

DISTINCTIVE FEATURES: wings with three clawed fingers

90

...PTERYX

Its name means:
ANCIENT WINGS

WHERE IT LIVED:

Europe

ITS WEIGHT:

2.2 lb. (1 kg)

ITS SIZE:

12–20 in. (30–50 cm) long

WHEN IT LIVED:

150–148 million years ago

| TRIASSIC | JURASSIC | CRETACEOUS |

All fossils of *Archaeopteryx* come from Germany. The first was found in 1861, and the most famous and well-preserved specimen was unearthed in 1874: a complete skeleton with clear feather impressions. The fossil looked like a cross between a dinosaur and a bird, and *Archaeopteryx*'s body was covered with plumage and flight feathers. It is owned and exhibited by Berlin's Natural History Museum and is known as the Berlin *Archaeopteryx*.

It was able to fly, although its wings still had three clearly visible fingers, each with a sharp claw. Its snout was very similar to a beak, but it was filled with small, pointed teeth. The tail was feathered and used to provide stability during flight, but it was made up of numerous vertebrae, just like those of dinosaurs.

It probably lived in trees, using its claws to climb up the trunks, and fly from tree to tree. It likely ate insects, worms, and carcasses.

PLUMAGE AND FEATHERS

Detailed studies of the fossils show that *Archaeopteryx*'s flight feathers and tail feathers were almost identical to those of today's birds. Its body feathers, on the other hand, were more like the strands found on other dinosaurs.

However, there was no plumage on the upper part of the neck and head. There are two hypotheses: some scientists think that *Archaeopteryx* had a bald head (like vultures), while most paleontologists are convinced that there were feathers on these areas that have not been preserved. They believed this because most *Archaeopteryx* fossils have been found on the ocean floor, transported there after they died. Remaining in water for such a long time would have caused the skin to soften and the small feathers that covered the head and neck to fall off while leaving the longer and more firmly attached plumage on the wings and tail intact.

A 3D SKELETON

For a long time, paleontologists wondered whether *Archaeopteryx* was able to fly or if it could only glide. Thanks to a three-dimensional reconstruction of the wing bones, it was possible to see that their bones were thinner than those of dinosaurs that moved on the ground and were more similar to those of today's birds, especially pheasants, which fly only in short bursts to overcome obstacles or escape predators.

Archaeopteryx was therefore capable of flight, but only for short distances, and it flapped its wings differently than birds. However, more studies are needed to understand exactly how it flapped them.

HERBIVOROUS D

> **The name means**
> **PLANT EATERS**

Herbivorous dinosaurs tended to be quadrupedal, although some could also move quickly on just their hind legs. They also had various forms of protection to defend themselves from predators. Some of these dinosaurs had enormous pointed horns, bony neck frills, spiky or club-shaped tails, skull armor, or bony plates covering their body. Others, however, had no defensive weapons other than their gigantic size. The long-necked sauropods were the largest land animals to have ever walked on our planet. Then there were the small and fast herbivores, which stayed in the undergrowth to search for food and hide from predators.

Because grass appeared toward the end of the Cretaceous, these dinosaurs mostly fed on other types of vegetation, such as leaves, ferns, and shrubs.

Only the last herbivorous dinosaurs were able to eat grass, and paleontologists have found evidence of this in some fossil excrements, called **coprolites**, found in India. Traces of grass—perhaps the first to appear on Earth—were found inside these remains, which probably belonged to a titanosaur (a "long-necked" dinosaur).

Some fossils of herbivorous dinosaurs, like those belonging to *Psittacosaurus*, an older and much smaller relative of *Triceratops*, show traces of primitive feathers like those found on carnivorous dinosaurs.

Like those of their meat-eating relatives, these would have helped maintain a constant body temperature and were displayed during the mating ritual. Horns or crested heads could also be used to impress females, and this is why scientists think they were brightly colored, like the beaks of today's birds.

NOSAURS

Herbivorous dinosaurs are the largest land animals to have ever walked on Earth. Thanks to their impressive necks and long tails, the gigantic sauropods could be longer than two buses. These reptiles would even make an elephant—the largest land animal in existence today—look really small.

HERBIVORES' TEETH

For mammals, it can generally be said that pointed teeth = carnivore and flat teeth = herbivore. However, where dinosaurs are concerned, herbivores almost never had flat teeth.

Each dinosaur developed different types of teeth, depending on the type of vegetation that was available. In fact, the teeth of herbivorous dinosaurs were all different shapes and sizes, and it was not unusual for them to have sharp, serrated surfaces.

Triceratops had very small teeth, about 2–2.5 inches (5–6 cm) long, including the root. They were triangular and had sharp edges, perfect for cutting the toughest and most fibrous plants. They were arranged in groups, with each consisting of about forty teeth. *Triceratops* had lots of teeth in its mouth, although few of them were functional or used for chewing at any one time.

***Triceratops* tooth with root**

An authentic reproduction of the tooth of the *Edmontosaurus*

Edmontosaurus, which belongs to the group of hadrosaurs, had over one thousand teeth similar in shape to those of *Triceratops*. But the teeth were narrower and longer, and arranged to create a large, rough surface—a kind of "grater" that allowed it to cut plants into very small pieces, making them easier to digest.

Camarasaurus, like other sauropods, had long, narrow, yet strong teeth with a strange spoon shape, and they were continually replaced so that they were always sharp and ready. They probably wore down due to the dinosaur endlessly stripping branches for the enormous amount of food it needed.

Tooth from a *Camarasaurus*

Rebbachisaurus, another sauropod, had peg-shaped teeth, which were very useful for raking leaves from trees. Its teeth were also self-sharpening! When *Rebbachisaurus* opened and closed its mouth, the upper and lower teeth rubbed together, sharpening the edges.

Tooth from a *Rebbachisaurus*

Teeth from an *Iguanodon*

Iguanodon even owes its name to its teeth. They are very similar to those of today's iguanas—slightly pointed but finely serrated, suitable for plants ranging from small shrubs to leaves on trees.

97

ALAMOS

Alamosaurus is part of the group of large sauropods. A skull of this dinosaur has never been found, but it is believed to be small compared to the size of the body. However, a few pencil-shaped teeth have been unearthed. They were used like a rake to tear the leaves off trees, but not for chewing. Also, polished stones have been found in the ribcages of several *Alamosaurus* skeletons. After being swallowed, the stones helped grind up food inside the stomach.

Alamosaurus was on Earth up to 66 million years ago and therefore existed until the end of the Mesozoic. This makes it the last sauropod, and one of the last dinosaurs, to live in North America before the great mass extinction.

DISTINCTIVE FEATURES:
long legs

AURUS

Its name means:
OJO ALAMO LIZARD

WHERE IT LIVED:

North America

ITS WEIGHT:

38 tons (34,000 kg)

ITS SIZE:

100 ft. (30 m) long

WHEN IT LIVED:

70–66 million years ago

TRIASSIC | JURASSIC | CRETACEOUS

EXTENSIVE MIGRATION?

All the large North American sauropods died out about 105 million years ago. But 35–40 million years later *Alamosaurus* seemed to appear out of nowhere! Its fossils were found in New Mexico in 1922, and then later in Utah, Wyoming, and Texas. Some paleontologists believe that *Alamosaurus* migrated to North America from South America when the two continents were joined by the Isthmus of Panama. This hypothesis is supported by the fact that *Alamosaurus* belongs to the family of titanosaurian sauropods, which were extremely common in South America during the Cretaceous.

THE GIANT OF BIG BEND

In 1999, some giant dinosaur bones were found sticking out from a hillside in Big Bend National Park in Texas. After careful digging, partial pelvic bones and ten neck vertebrae of an adult *Alamosaurus* were found. This specimen appears to have been huge, measuring just over 100 feet (30 m). Due to their huge size and the remote location of the site, removing these bones by hand was impossible, so the park gave special permission to use a helicopter!

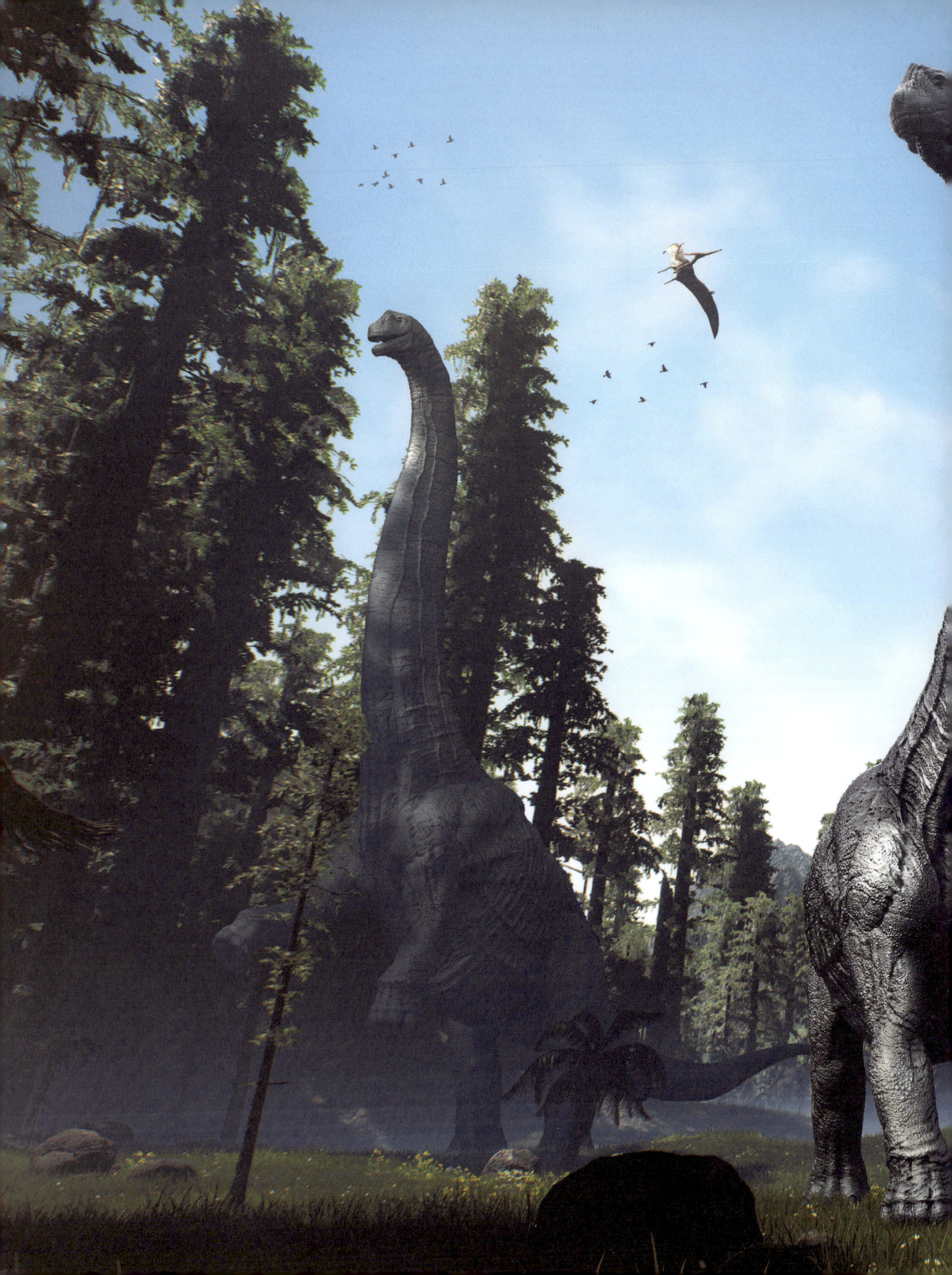

Three examples of *Alamosauruses*

PUERTAS

Puertasaurus reuili is probably one of the largest sauropod dinosaurs ever found. It was first described in 2005 and is named after Pablo Puerta and Santiago Reuil, the two fossil hunters who discovered it in 2001.

DISTINCTIVE FEATURES:
enormous vertebrae

The only remains to have been found are four vertebrae: a neck vertebra, a dorsal vertebra, and two tail vertebrae. These bones are only 3% of the skeleton, and only the dorsal vertebra is complete. What impressed paleontologists the most is the size of the bones: the largest is 3.5 feet (1.06 m) long and 5.5 feet (1.68 m) wide. These dimensions make it the largest sauropod vertebra found to date. Its neck must have been flexible enough for it to reach branches above it, as high as 50 feet (15 m), without having to move its entire body.

...AURUS

Its name means:
PUERTA'S LIZARD

WHERE IT LIVED:

South America

ITS WEIGHT:

45–55 tons
(40,000–49,000 kg)

ITS SIZE:

100 ft. (30 m) long

WHEN IT LIVED:

83–66 million years ago

| TRIASSIC | JURASSIC | CRETACEOUS |

ESTIMATED SIZE

Since there are very few remains of *Puertasaurus*, it is difficult to reconstruct what this dinosaur looked like. Its length and weight are based on other similar, more complete dinosaurs, such as *Argentinosaurus* and *Futalognkosaurus*. Even so, it is never easy to guess the weight, since soft tissue like muscle and fat are almost never preserved. Paleontologists have changed their idea of its weight several times, going from 100 tons to 60 tons, and more recently to 45–55 tons.

TRICERA

Triceratops is the most famous herbivorous dinosaur, just like *T. rex* is the most famous carnivore. Did you know that *Triceratops* also shared its habitat with the fearsome predator and was probably one of its favorite prey? When *Triceratops* was first discovered in 1887, the famous paleontologist Othniel Charles Marsh mistook it for a prehistoric bison. In his defense, Marsh only had the upper part of the skull, which had only two of the three horns. More importantly, Marsh thought that the surrounding rocks were less than 3 million years old, which would have made it impossible for it to be a dinosaur. The paleontologist only changed his mind after other specimens were discovered. Today, there are many dozens of specimens of *Triceratops*, from hatchlings to elderly individuals.

In addition to the two forward-facing horns just above the eyes, *Triceratops* has a third, smaller horn above its large, round nostrils. At the back of the massive skull, there is a **bony frill**.

DISTINCTIVE FEATURES: three horns and a fan-shaped frill

TOPS

Its name means:
THREE-HORNED FACE

WHERE IT LIVED:

North America

The front of its mouth formed a beak. It had up to 800 teeth arranged in columns of up to 5 stacked teeth, which created an irregular surface for eating tough, fibrous vegetables. The huge number of *Triceratops* fossils shows how sturdy its bones were to be preserved so well, and also how common this dinosaur was in its time.

ITS WEIGHT:

9–10 tons (8,200–9,000 kg)

ITS SIZE:

26–30 ft. (8–9 m) long

WHEN IT LIVED:

68–66 million years ago

| TRIASSIC | JURASSIC | CRETACEOUS |

DEFENSIVE, OFFENSIVE, OR ORNAMENTAL?

Triceratops's distinctive horns and large bony frill were immediately believed to have been used as weapons to defend itself against predators or in fights with members of its own species. These hypotheses came from the discovery of signs of wounds on the horns and frill. Today, however, some of these wounds are thought to be from disease. New studies on the bone structure of the frill, horns, and skull showed they were covered with layers of keratin (like our nails), and this changed beliefs about the function of the frill and horns. The head and beak of many of today's birds also have this type of coating on very colorful areas. *Triceratops*, like other related dinosaurs, was likely much more colorful than we thought and the frill and horns were likely an ornament used for recognizing its own species, communication, and visual display during courtship.

SOCIAL, BUT NOT TOO MUCH

For a long time, it was believed that *Triceratops* lived in **herds**, similar to those of rhinos, working together to protect the young. Unfortunately, there is no real evidence of *Triceratops* being a social animal like other ceratopsids (horned dinosaurs). Although many *Triceratops* fossils have been found, groups of specimens have only been found at a couple of sites: three juveniles in Montana, and two adults, whose sex is unknown, and a hatchling in Wyoming.

TOROSA

DISTINCTIVE FEATURES: a very long frill at the back

URUS

Its name means: PERFORATED LIZARD

WHERE IT LIVED:

North America

ITS WEIGHT:

4.5–6.5 tons (4,000–6,000 kg)

ITS SIZE:

26–30 ft. (8–9 m) long

WHEN IT LIVED:

68–66 million years ago

| TRIASSIC | JURASSIC | CRETACEOUS |

Torosaurus belongs to the family Ceratopsidae, the horned-faced dinosaurs, of which *Triceratops* is also a member. The two have a few characteristics in common, such as the two horns above the eyes and the bony frill extending from the back of the skull over the neck and shoulders. However, *Torosaurus*'s frill had two large holes in it and was much larger. The skull could reach an incredible length of over 9 feet (2.8 m), making it one of the largest known land animal skulls. The nasal horn was also different: *Torosaurus*'s was very small, if not almost absent. Its name is often translated as "bull lizard," due to the Latin word *taurus*, but when paleontologist Othniel Charles Marsh chose its name in 1891, he was probably thinking of the Greek word *toreo*, which means "to perforate." Unfortunately, he never explained the true meaning of the name. *Torosaurus*'s horns and frill, like the *Triceratops*, are also believed to have functioned in visual display among its own species, so they were probably very colorful. However, the holes in the frill were likely not visible and were covered in skin when the animal was alive.

TOROSAURUS OR TRICERATOPS?

Some paleontologists have a theory that *Torosaurus* is actually an adult *Triceratops*. They think that the frill grew larger with age and that the two holes were a way to make it lighter. Other scholars don't agree with this hypothesis because if it were true, there would be no juvenile *Torosauruses*, and yet a skull found in the 19th century and analyzed again recently has characteristics that are not of an adult. So at least for now these ceratopsids are still considered two separate dinosaurs.

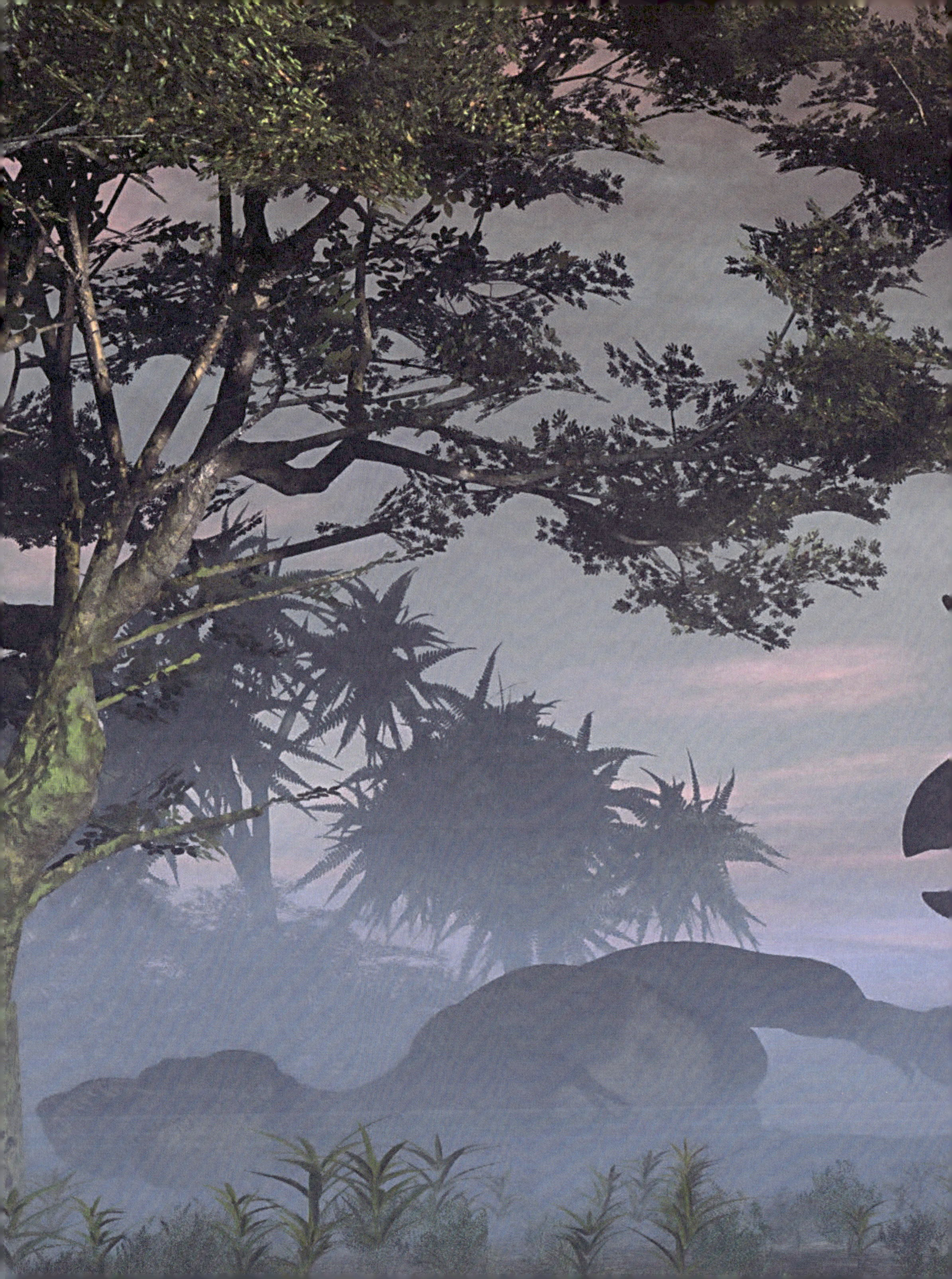

Even a predator like *Tyrannosaurus* can be taken down by the defensive weapons of its prey

EINIOSA

Einiosaurus's most distinctive feature was its large, forward-curving nasal horn, which was completely different from those of all the other dinosaurs in its group. It also had a bony neck frill with a pair of long backward-curving spikes, but the two rounded brow horns were so low that they were barely visible. The strange horn on its snout was perhaps used as a defensive weapon or for mating displays. Paleontologists have suggested that the neck frill, which was probably covered with brightly colored keratin (like that of *Triceratops*), may also have been displayed in mating rituals or that it helped individuals recognize other dinosaurs of the same species. Since the frill had two large holes, it wasn't solid enough to be an effective shield. Still, it may have scared off predators, and its spikes would have protected it in combat.

DISTINCTIVE FEATURES:
a forward-facing horn

URUS

Its name means:
BUFFALO LIZARD

WHERE IT LIVED:

North America

ITS WEIGHT:

1.4 tons (1,300 kg)

ITS SIZE:

15 ft. (4.5 m) long

WHEN IT LIVED:

74 million years ago

| TRIASSIC | JURASSIC | CRETACEOUS |

LIVING IN A HERD

Einiosaurus was first discovered in Montana (United States) in 1985. The paleontologists were actually on their way to another excavation site in search of a different dinosaur (*Maiasaura*), but at the last moment the owner of the land refused to allow them onto his property. But since they were forced to choose a different site, the team unearthed three complete adult skulls and numerous other bones belonging to both old and young specimens. The large number of bones suggested that an entire *Einiosaurus* herd had died there. Paleontologists believe that this dinosaur lived in large herds, like bison or wildebeest do today.

Three *Einiosauruses*, which usually lived in large herds

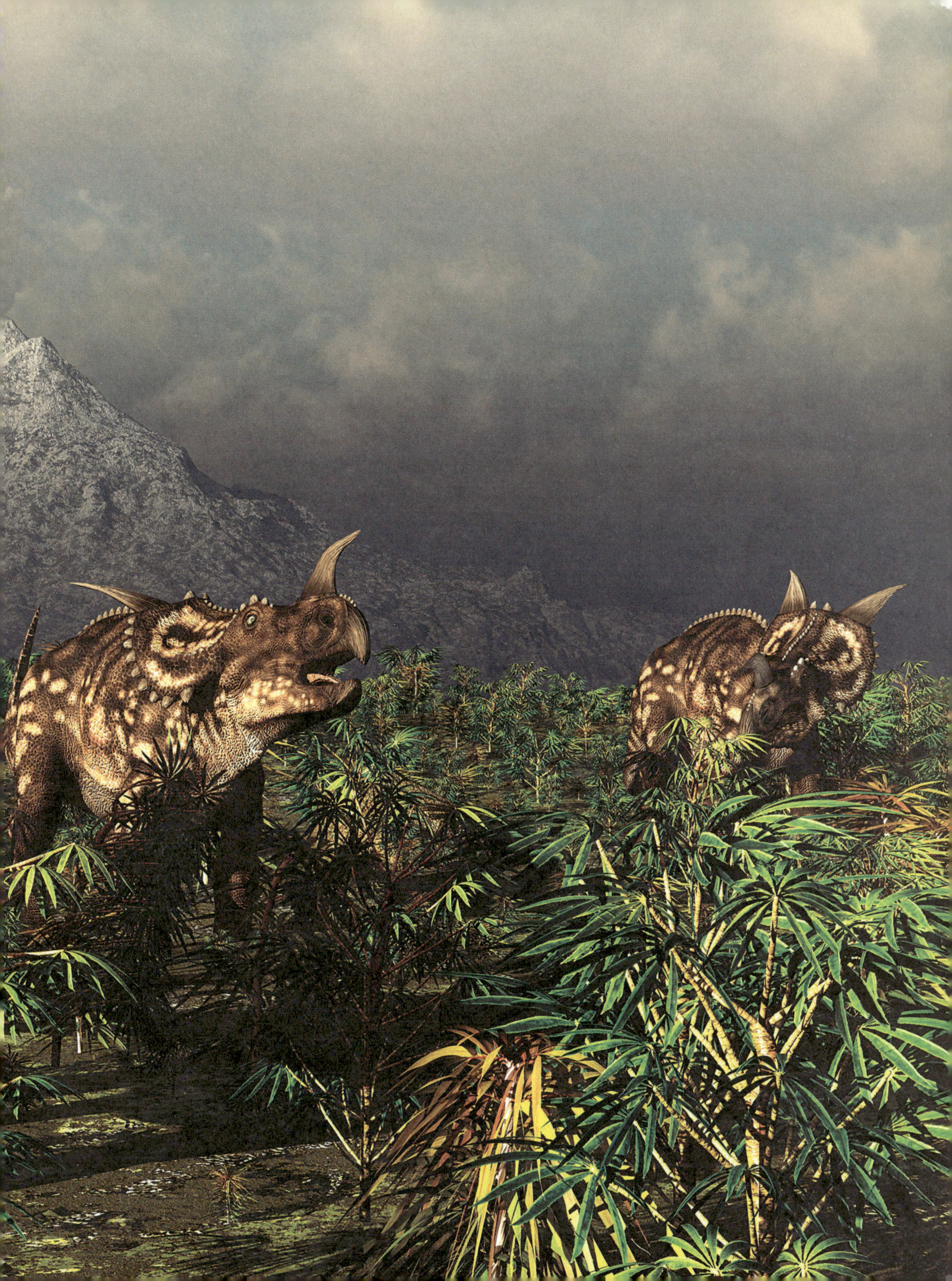

DIABLOC

Not much is known about this dinosaur, since there are only two known *Diabloceratops* fossils. The first was discovered in 1998, and the second in 2002, both in a layer of sandstone in the Wahweap Formation in the state of Utah. Both fossils are only the skull and have the typical features of all ceratopsids (horned dinosaurs like *Triceratops*): a neck frill, two horns above the eyes, a small horn on top of the snout, and a mouth that ends with a beak useful for cropping vegetation and has teeth similar to those of *Triceratops*, which it used to grind its food.

DISTINCTIVE FEATURES: a crest with two horns

ERATOPS

Its name means:
DEVIL-HORNED FACE

WHERE IT LIVED:

North America

ITS WEIGHT:

maximum 2 tons (1,800 kg)

ITS SIZE:

16–20 ft. (5–6 m) long

WHEN IT LIVED:

81–76 million years ago

| TRIASSIC | JURASSIC | CRETACEOUS |

The shape and appearance of its neck frill makes *Diabloceratops* a special ceratopsid. The frill wasn't fan-shaped like those of other horned dinosaurs, but narrower, with two big holes and a large pair of upward and sideways-curving horns on the back.

The two paleontologists who studied the discovered fossils in 2010 were inspired by these two horns when they named the dinosaur. Although the description is based on the skull, the rest of the skeleton and general appearance of *Diabloceratops*'s body has been guessed from those of related dinosaurs.

Diabloceratops was about the same size as a large male white rhinoceros (*Ceratotherium simum*). Despite the similarities, the first is a reptile, while the second is a mammal. It is quite common for similar shapes or structures—in this case, the horns—to develop in species belonging to very different groups.

A CROWDED ENVIRONMENT

The type of rock in which the two *Diabloceratops* skulls were found suggests that Utah was a humid area at that time—a vast plain filled with rivers and lakes. This type of habitat can be home to various animal and plant species. In fact, numerous other fossils have been unearthed from the same layers of rock that preserved the remains of *Diabloceratops*, revealing that it was a very lush and crowded environment. Many other dinosaurs have been found, including *Ankylosaurus* (armored dinosaurs) and even a *Tyrannosaur*, which was probably the most feared predator. There were also fish, turtles, and mammals similar to rodents and kangaroos.

PROTOCE

Even at quick glance, it is impossible not to notice how much *Protoceratops* looked like *Triceratops*. However, *Protoceratops* doesn't belong to the family Ceratopsidae (horned dinosaurs), but to the family **Protoceratopsidae**. In fact, it was the first member of the family to be found, hence its name.

RATOPS

Its name means:
FIRST HORNED FACE

WHERE IT LIVED:

Asia

ITS WEIGHT:

176–200 lb. (80–90 kg)

ITS SIZE:

6 ft. (1.8 m) long

DISTINCTIVE FEATURES:
extremely large skull compared to the body

WHEN IT LIVED:

75–72 million years ago

| TRIASSIC | JURASSIC | CRETACEOUS |

Protoceratops was a small dinosaur, especially when compared to *Triceratops* or *Torosaurus*, although it had a very large skull, with a huge beak and a neck frill with very wide holes. Also, there were no horns above the eyes. Right now there are only two known species of *Protoceratops*. The larger one had a slightly wider neck frill and more pronounced cheekbones, as well as two small ridges that ran along the upper edge of the beak. Both species of *Protoceratops* were quadrupeds, like their larger relatives, but they had thinner legs that were better for running. Thanks to their beak and teeth, which were arranged to form an irregular surface, they wouldn't have had any problems eating tough, fibrous vegetation.

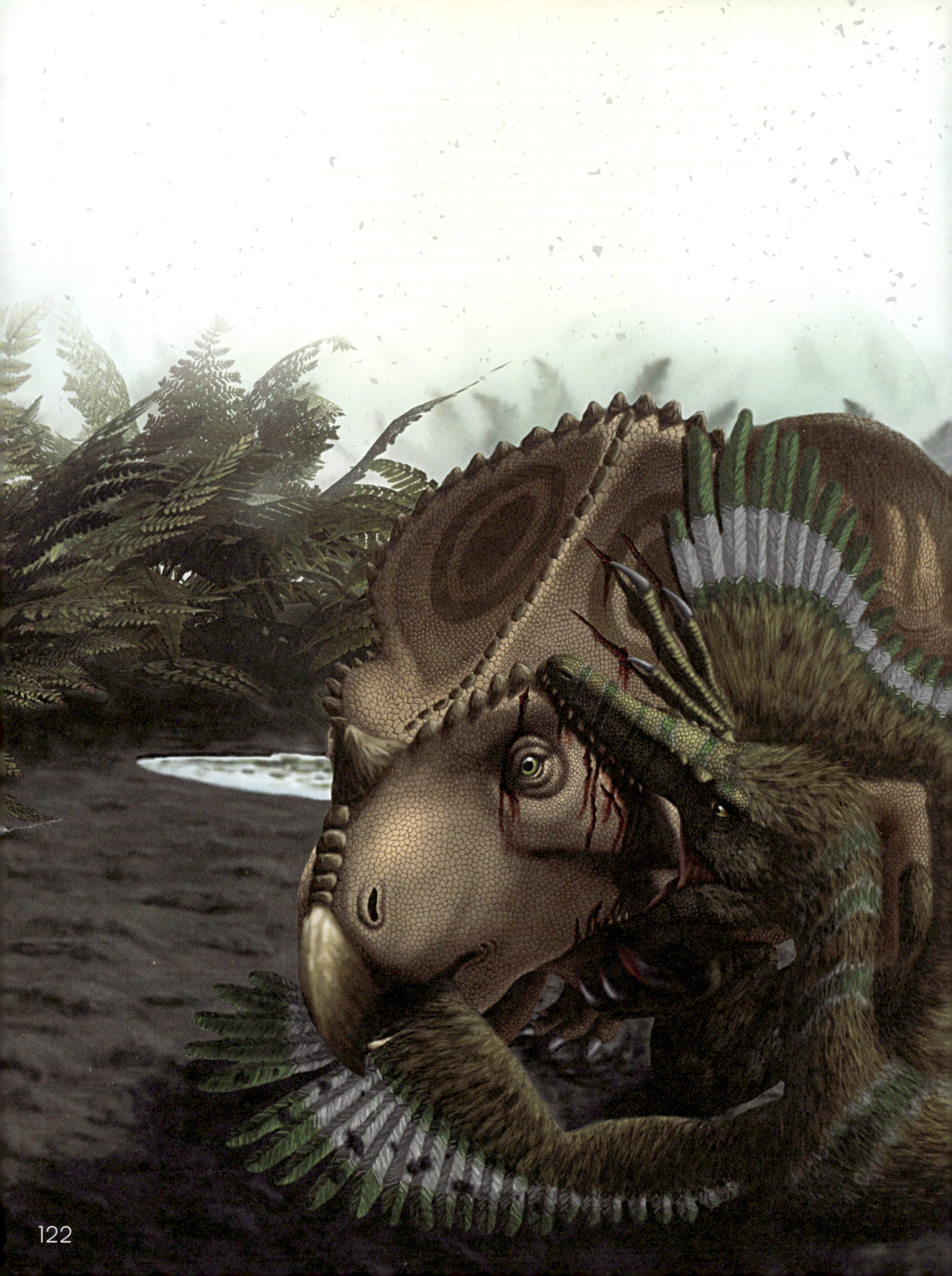

The large number of *Protoceratops* fossils found, in the sand of the Gobi Desert in Mongolia, and often several specimens of different ages in the same place, has allowed scholars to hypothesize that they lived in herds. In the 1920s, some eggs were also found, and for seventy years it was believed they belonged to *Protoceratops*. But in 1993 they were discovered to be *Oviraptor* eggs. In the early 2000s, a few nests containing *Protoceratops* hatchlings at different stages of growth were found. This discovery helped to establish that they were social animals, and they took care of the hatchlings in the early stages of life.

Fossils of *Protoceratops* skeletons are often so well preserved that we can observe even the most delicate structures—for example, **sclerotic rings**, or bony structures around the eye sockets, which supported and protected the eyeball. By studying these bones and eye sockets, the size of the eyes has been estimated to have had a diameter of about 2 inches (5 cm).

Animals with such large eyes are usually active at night, but more recent studies have shown that *Protoceratops* was actually active in short bursts throughout the day. The famous fossil of a *Velociraptor* (mainly active at night) with its claw in the throat of a *Protoceratops*, whose beak is biting its attacker's arm, found in 1971, has frozen in time a fight that probably took place at dusk.

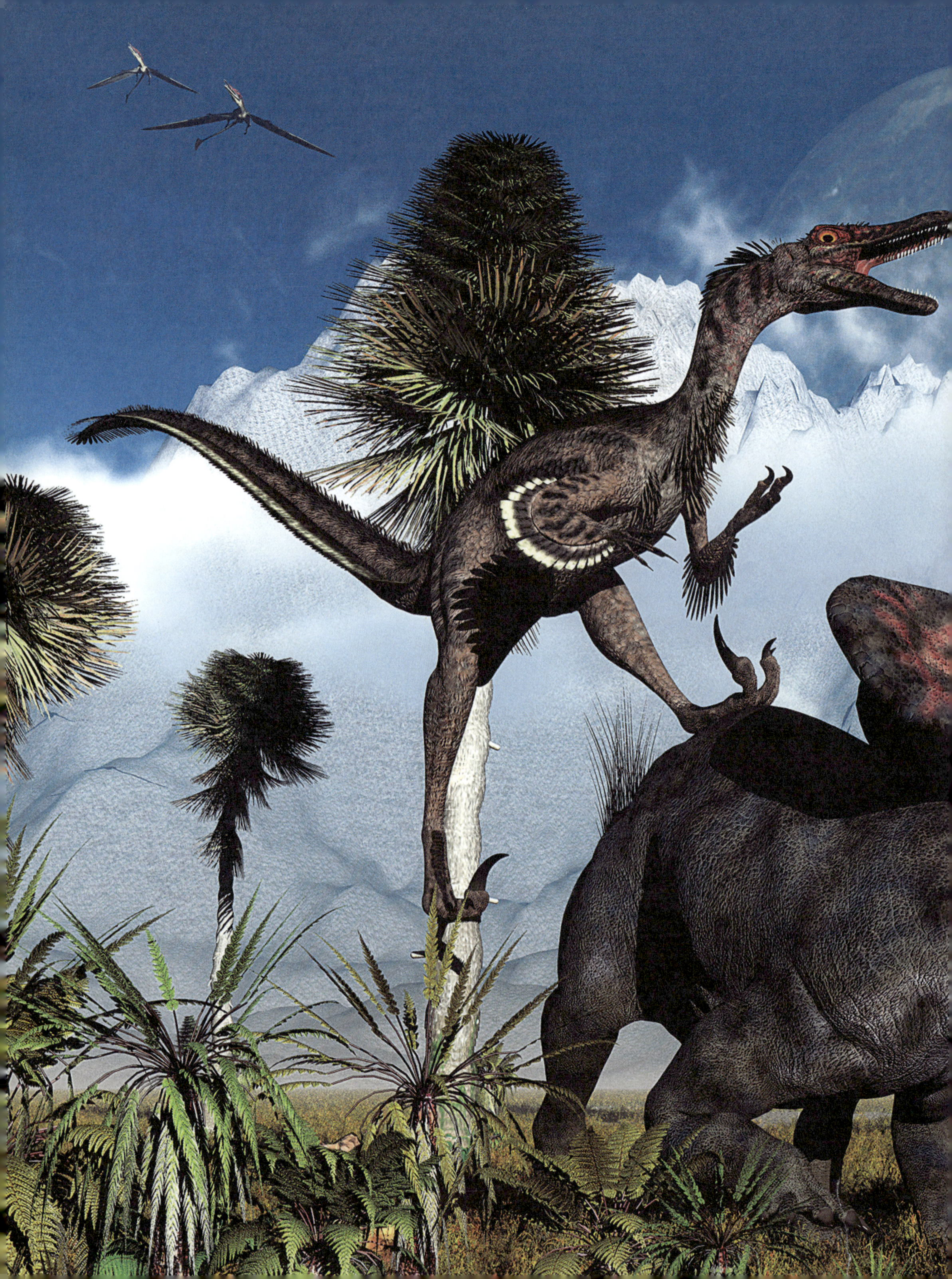

A pair of *Velociraptors* unleash their deadly claws on a *Protoceratops*

PACHYRHI

Instead of horns, *Pachyrhinosaurus* had clumps of flattened bones on top of its head: a large one on the snout and a smaller one above the eyes. Its large, lumpy nose, which was more noticeable in older males, is what makes this dinosaur unique.

By studying the inside of the bone, paleontologists found strong similarities to the forehead of an adult male musk oxen. They believe that the bump on *Pachyrinosaurus*'s head was also covered by a thick pad of hardened skin, which would have helped absorb the blows in fights.

DISTINCTIVE FEATURES: a large bump on its snout

NOSAURUS

Its name means: THICK-NOSED LIZARD

WHERE IT LIVED:

North America

Pachyrhinosaurus ate vegetation, which it would crop with its mighty beak and then shred with the sharp teeth in the back of its mouth. And as soon as a tooth wore down, it fell out and was replaced by a new one.

ITS WEIGHT:

4 tons (3,600 kg)

ITS SIZE:

26 ft. (8 m) long

WHEN IT LIVED:

73.5–68.5 million years ago

| TRIASSIC | JURASSIC | CRETACEOUS |

BONE BED

Pachyrhinosaurus lived in groups, at least in certain times of the year, since groups of individuals of different ages have been discovered in the same place. In fact, several *Pachyrhinosaurus* bone beds have been discovered. These sites have large numbers of fossils. In Pipestone Creek, in Canada, 14 skulls and 3,500 bones were found, and paleontologists think that the herd died while trying to cross a river during a flood. The skeletons belong to four different age groups, ranging from adult specimens to juveniles. This would suggest that *Pachyrhinosaurus* raised and took care of its young.

Three *Pachyrhinosaurus perotum*, the species living most north. They had slower growth during the cold winters

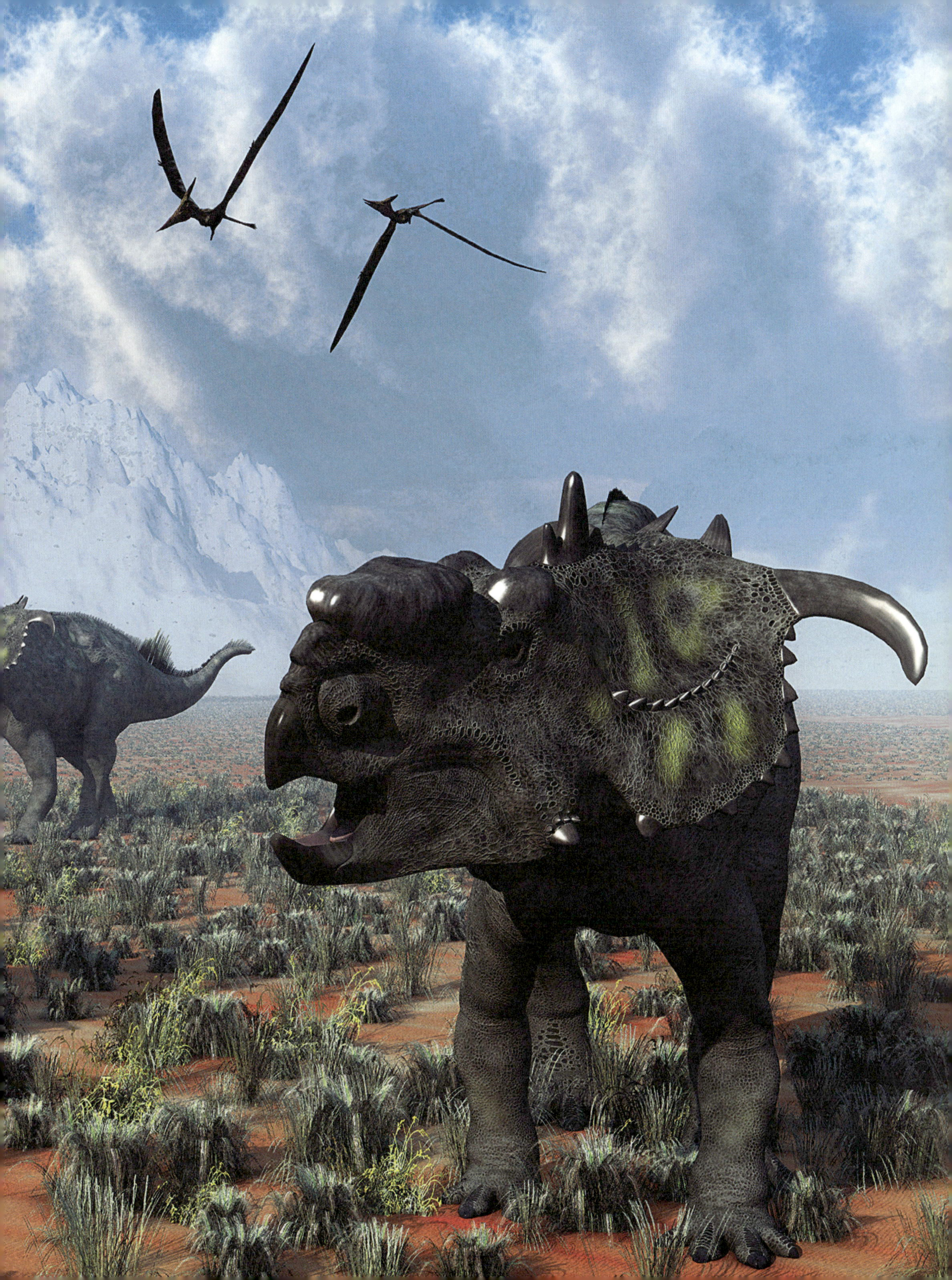

DIPLODO

Diplodocus is one of the most famous and well-known long-necked dinosaurs among paleontologists, since it is one of the few sauropods that we have an almost complete skeleton of.

Although North America was ruled by large herbivores during the Jurassic, there were still plenty of ferocious predators, such as *Ceratosaurus* and *Allosaurus*. *Diplodocus* was able to defend itself with its enormous size. If necessary, it could stand up on its hind legs and try to crush its opponent or wound it by striking it with the large, sharp thumb claws on its front feet.

Another possible weapon was the sound of its tail, which tapered at the tip like a whip. *Diplodocus* could swing the tip of its tail at speeds of 5–8 feet (1.5–2.5 m) per second. Its tail made a cracking sound that was 2,000 times louder than that of a whip. These cracks could be heard from a long distance and would have frightened off predators. However, the tail was probably not used as a weapon, since the impact would have seriously damaged it.

CUS

Its name means:
DOUBLE BEAM

WHERE IT LIVED:

North America

ITS WEIGHT:

10–16 tons (9,000–14,000 kg)

ITS SIZE:

108 ft. (33 m) long

WHEN IT LIVED:

154–152 million years ago

| TRIASSIC | JURASSIC | CRETACEOUS |

DISTINCTIVE FEATURES:
long tail with a very thin tip

In 2010, the skull of a young *Diplodocus* was noted to be quite different than an adult skull. The main differences were the shape of the snout and the position of the teeth, which were not only in the front of the mouth of the young dinosaur. This suggests that the adults and young probably ate in different ways. Standing up on its hind legs and using its tail as a support, an adult *Diplodocus* could reach vegetation as high as 36 feet (11 m). It would then tear the leaves with its peg-like front teeth that stuck out..

DIPLODOCUS DISCOVERIES

Our sense of *Diplodocus*'s posture has changed a lot over the years because of new discoveries by paleontologists that helped improve our understanding of the skeleton.

One of the first reconstructions, from 1910, depicts two specimens on a riverbank with their legs spread out, similar to those of a lizard. The discovery of some sauropod footprints in the 1930s, however, revealed that *Diplodocus* had straight legs under its body, just like all other dinosaurs.

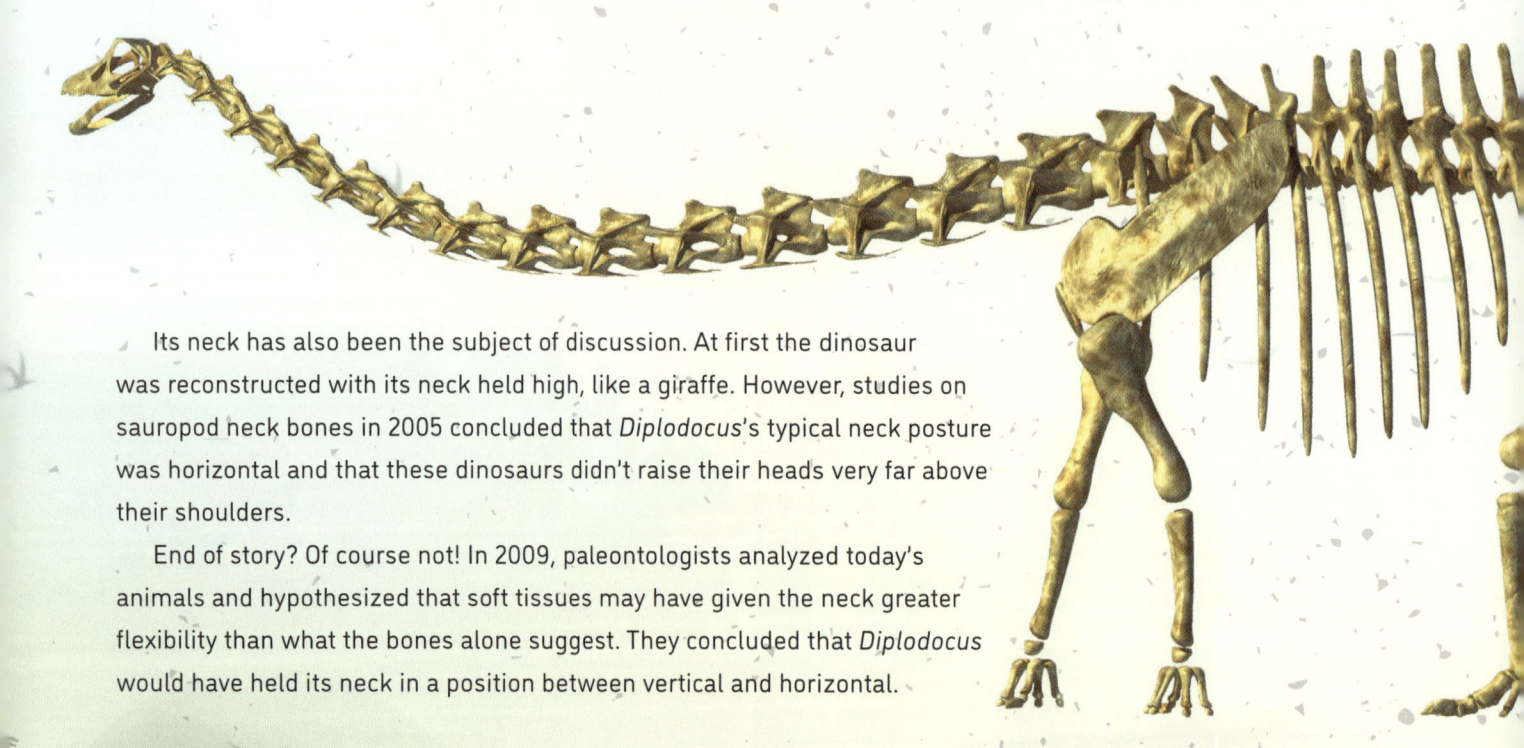

Its neck has also been the subject of discussion. At first the dinosaur was reconstructed with its neck held high, like a giraffe. However, studies on sauropod neck bones in 2005 concluded that *Diplodocus*'s typical neck posture was horizontal and that these dinosaurs didn't raise their heads very far above their shoulders.

End of story? Of course not! In 2009, paleontologists analyzed today's animals and hypothesized that soft tissues may have given the neck greater flexibility than what the bones alone suggest. They concluded that *Diplodocus* would have held its neck in a position between vertical and horizontal.

Illustration of a horizontal neck position. The skeleton above shows the most recent understanding of *Diplodocus*'s posture

Many sauropods laid all their eggs in large **nesting areas,** digging a few deep holes that they then covered with vegetation. It is possible that *Diplodocus* did the same thing.

Furthermore, the eggs were very small compared to the size of the dinosaur, and this could have reduced the risk of the eggs being eaten by another species. Large eggs took longer to hatch and would be more at risk.

APATOSA

Apatosaurus had legs that were sturdier and not as long as other sauropods, and its hind legs were larger than its front legs. Like most sauropods, *Apatosaurus* had only one large claw on each of its front feet. Its tail was long and unusually thin, like a whip. Paleontologists made a computer model of it and discovered that the cracking sound of the tip would have produced a sound similar to a cannon shot, which could be heard from miles away. However, the thin tip would not have been able to injure predators, so its tail could not be used as a defensive weapon.

Apatosaurus's neck was very large and sturdy, but a system of air pockets made it lighter than you might think. *Apatosaurus* had a small skull for its body size and had teeth shaped like chisels. This dinosaur probably fed mainly on vegetation low to the ground, but its long neck would also have allowed it to eat tender leaves on taller trees. *Apatosaurus* probably ate about 880 pounds (400 kg) of vegetation a day, without chewing it, at the same time ingesting stones called **gastroliths** that helped grind up food in the dinosaur's stomach.

DISTINCTIVE FEATURES: a long, thin tail

...URUS

Its name means:
DECEPTIVE LIZARD

WHERE IT LIVED:

North America

ITS WEIGHT:

20 tons (18,000 kg)

ITS SIZE:

69–75 ft. (21–23 m) long

WHEN IT LIVED:

155–150 million years ago

TRIASSIC | JURASSIC | CRETACEOUS

A DECEPTIVE REPTILE

The name *Apatosaurus* was coined in 1877 by paleontologist Othniel Charles Marsh, based on an almost complete skeleton discovered in the Rocky Mountains in Colorado (United States). The term comes from the Greek word *apatè*, which means "deceit" or "deceitful." Marsh gave it this name based on the bones on the underside of the tail, which are more like those of mosasaurs (marine reptiles) than other dinosaurs.

PACHYCEPH

Pachycephalosaurus had an extremely thick skull, with the upper part of the head up to 9 inches (23 cm) thick. The domed skull was so hefty that sometimes it is the only part of the skeleton preserved as a fossil.

Some paleontologists have speculated that the thickened skull of *Pachycephalosaurus* was used for ferocious head-to-head battles between males, perhaps during the mating period, just like some animals today. However, there are some scientists who think that this dinosaur's neck vertebrae weren't strong enough to not to break in such fights. Also, given the spongy texture of the bone, the domes would not have been severely damaged by direct blows. Still, the numerous scars found on fossils suggest that *Pachycephalosaurus* did fight in head-to-head combat. It is also thought that the dome had an outer layer of keratin that would have protected it against damage caused by headbutting.

DISTINCTIVE FEATURES: a bony dome on its head

ALOSAURUS

Its name means:
THICK-HEADED LIZARD

WHERE IT LIVED:

North America

ITS WEIGHT:

990 lb. (450 kg)

ITS SIZE:

15 ft. (4.5 m) long

WHEN IT LIVED:

70–66 million years ago

| TRIASSIC | JURASSIC | CRETACEOUS |

The complete jawbone of a juvenile *Pachycephalosaurus* was found in 2018, which puzzled paleontologists. It had the same broad, leaf-shaped teeth in the back of its mouth as all other specimens, good for crushing tough plants, fruit, and seeds. But it also had sharp triangular teeth only at the front, similar to those of some carnivorous dinosaurs. Paleontologists don't know whether *Pachycephalosaurus* had these teeth only when it was young or if it kept them throughout its life. Maybe perhaps young *Pachycephalosaurs* were omnivorous, while adults ate just plants.

Paleontologists have found only skulls of these dinosaurs. This skeleton is how they believe the rest of the body would have looked

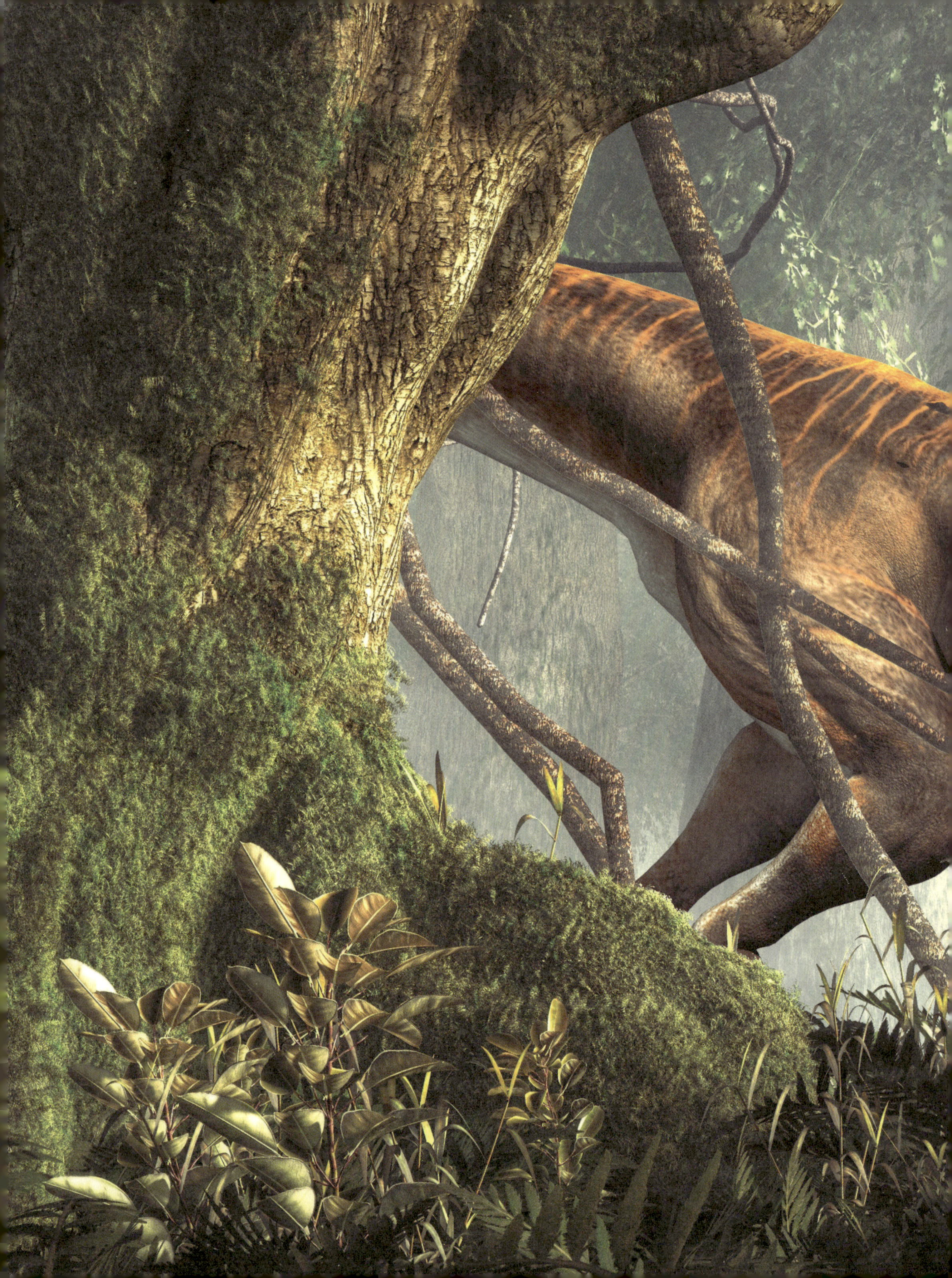

A *Pachycephalosaurus* leaning forward in an "aggressive" posture, ready to use its head to fight

STYGIMO

Stygimoloch is a dinosaur belonging to the family Pachycephalosauridae. Like other members of this family, it had a very thick skull dome, although it was smaller and shaped a bit like a pear. The rest of the skull was covered with bony bumps and clusters of spikes. There were a few small spikes on the front of the snout, above the nose, and a pair of large spikes (up to 6 inches [15 cm]) on the back corners. It had a bipedal posture, a broad chest, and a very stiff tail, especially the tip. Like all pachycephalosaurs, it had very short arms.

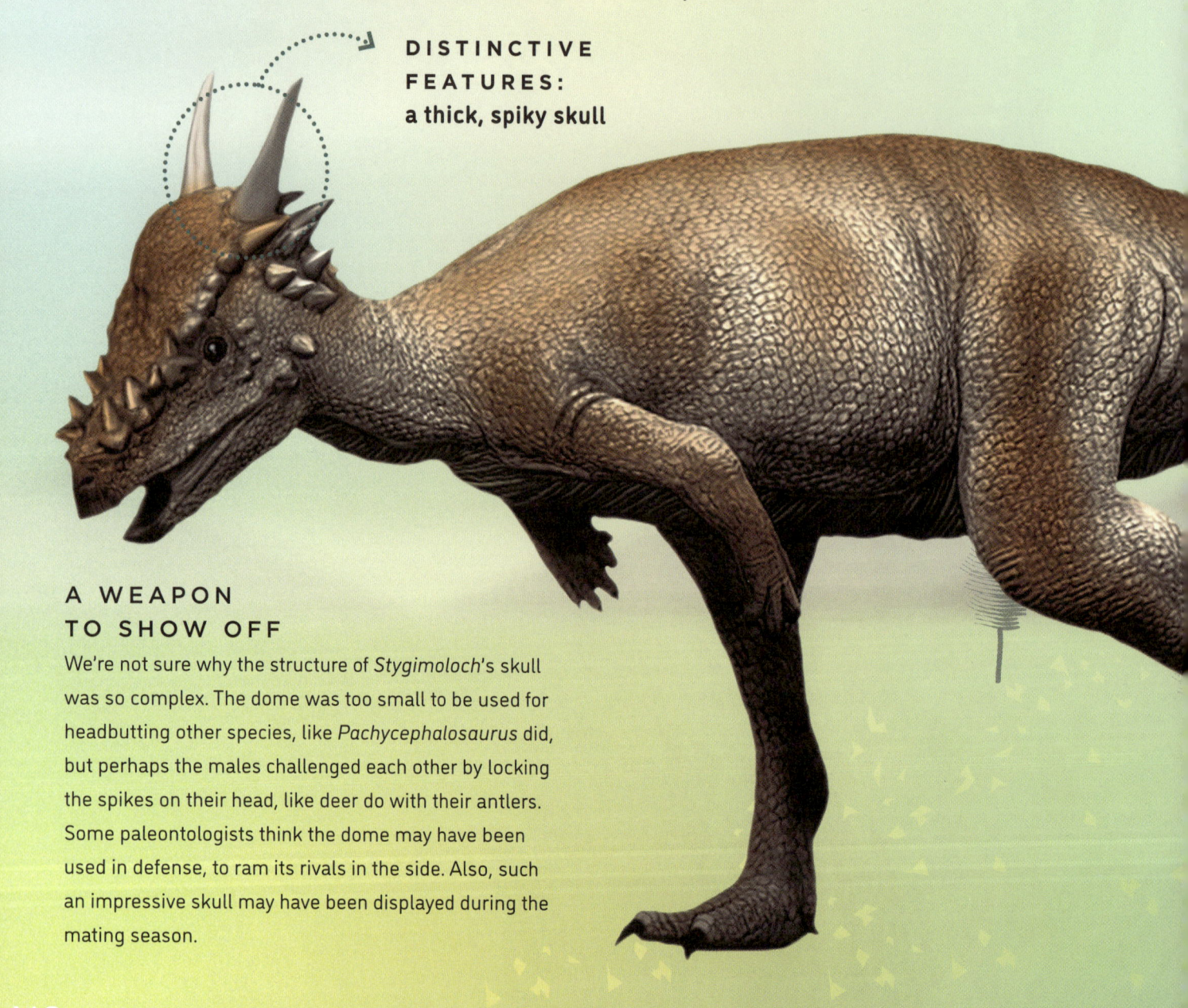

DISTINCTIVE FEATURES: a thick, spiky skull

A WEAPON TO SHOW OFF

We're not sure why the structure of *Stygimoloch*'s skull was so complex. The dome was too small to be used for headbutting other species, like *Pachycephalosaurus* did, but perhaps the males challenged each other by locking the spikes on their head, like deer do with their antlers. Some paleontologists think the dome may have been used in defense, to ram its rivals in the side. Also, such an impressive skull may have been displayed during the mating season.

LOCH

Its name means:
DEMON FROM THE RIVER STYX

WHERE IT LIVED:

North America

ITS WEIGHT:

220 lb. (100 kg)

ITS SIZE:

up to 10 ft. (3 m) long

WHEN IT LIVED:

70–66 million years ago

| TRIASSIC | JURASSIC | CRETACEOUS |

THREE DINOSAURS, OR JUST ONE?

Not only was *Stygimoloch* found in the same places as *Pachycephalosaurus*, the skull bones of both dinosaurs had the same structure and could have changed shape as they grew, losing horns as well as growing the dome as they matured. This is why some paleontologists think that *Stygimoloch* was actually just a young *Pachycephalosaurus*. An additional reason was that only adult *Pachycephalosaurus* skulls and only juvenile *Stygimoloch* were found in the same area. But that's not all. There was another pachycephalosaur even smaller than *Stygimoloch*, called *Dracorex*, that also had a spiky head but not the typical thickened skull, and it could be an even younger *Pachycephalosaurus*.

MAIASA

Maiasaura was a hadrosaur or one of the duck-billed dinosaurs. Like other hadrosaurs, *Maiasaura* was a quadrupedal herbivore, with a small skull compared to the size of its body, a very arched back, and a very straight, muscular tail.

This dinosaur became famous because of the huge number of fossils found recently. It all began in 1978, when an entire nest was discovered in a fossil-filled site in Montana. The nest was a circular structure containing fragments of eggshells and the remains of a few hatchlings. What sparked paleontologists' interest the most was that the young dinosaurs were still in the nest, despite being far too large to have just hatched from their eggs.

This could mean that these dinosaurs remained in the nest for a long time after they emerged from eggs, and that their parents took care of them by bringing food.

Many more nests were discovered that contained dozens of eggs as large as those of ostriches and hundreds of specimens at different growth stages. The hypothesis that they were taken care of by their parents was supported by the discovery that the leg bones of newborn *Maiasaura* hatchlings were not strong enough for walking.

URA

Its name means:
GOOD LIZARD MOTHER

WHERE IT LIVED:

North America

ITS WEIGHT:

2–3 tons (1,800–2,700 kg)

ITS SIZE:

30 ft. (9 m) long

WHEN IT LIVED:

77–76 million years ago

| TRIASSIC | JURASSIC | CRETACEOUS |

DISTINCTIVE FEATURES:
a snout with a beak

This, together with the signs of wear on their teeth, proved that the adults brought them food. They seemed to stay in the nest for as long as one year. The hatchlings walked primarily as bipeds, shifting to a quadrupedal posture as they grew. Another important discovery was that the nests were never found alone, but in large colonies. The nests were about 23–26 feet (7–8 m) apart, the smallest space the adults needed for going easily back and forth with food for the hatchlings and also replenishing the nest with vegetation that—as it **decomposed**—maintained the correct temperature for the unhatched eggs.

These findings helped paleontologists learn that *Maiasaura* was a social dinosaur. It moved in herds of hundreds, or perhaps thousands, of individuals. The presence of so many herbivores would have made it necessary to constantly move in search of food, so it is possible that *Maiasaura* made seasonal migrations. During these long journeys, they would have encountered many other dinosaurs, including predators such as *Daspletosaurus*, a cousin of *T. rex*. The only way to defend themselves would have been by moving in large herds—there's strength in numbers!

A 3D reconstruction of a *Maiasaura*'s nest

ANKYLOS

The first *Ankylosaurus* fossils were found in 1906 by American paleontologist Barnum Brown, nicknamed Mr. Bones. He pulled a partial skull, two teeth, part of a shoulder, some vertebrae, and more than thirty bony plates called osteoderms from the rocks in the fossil-rich Hell Creek Formation in Montana. That is where many fossils of *Tyrannosaurus* and *Triceratops* have also been found.

Some researchers think that the tail club was composed of tightly interlocking vertebrae with a large bony ball on the end

However, these bones were not enough to reconstruct the dinosaur's appearance. Only thanks to later findings have we been able to make a reliable reconstruction. *Ankylosaurus* was a quadrupedal dinosaur with a very short and squat body supported by four strong legs. It had a triangular skull and a stiff tail ending in a large club-like structure.

Other researchers think that at the end of the tail there are two large and two smaller horizontal bone structures

AURUS

Its name means:
FUSED LIZARD

WHERE IT LIVED:

North America

DISTINCTIVE FEATURES:
body armor and a tail club

ITS WEIGHT:

5.3–8.8 tons (4,800–8,000 kg)

ITS SIZE:

20–26 ft. (6–8 m) long

WHEN IT LIVED:

68–66 million years ago

| TRIASSIC | JURASSIC | CRETACEOUS |

The entire body was armored, thanks to the osteoderms that completely covered it. Paleontologists think that this armor was able to resist the bites of large predators. The skull was also armored, but its scaly appearance was due not to osteoderms but to a change of the bone structure that led to all the skull bones being fused together. The back of the head was much wider than the front and had two pyramid-shaped horns extending backward from each corner. It had a highly developed nasal cavity, which some paleontologists believe was used to make sounds for communicating. This hypothesis, although not entirely accepted, is supported by studies of the inner ear, which appears to have been able to hear the type of sounds produced by the nasal cavity.

The *Ankylosaurus*'s mouth contained several dozen teeth shaped like a serrated leaf, although much smaller. These teeth and the beak at the front of the mouth allowed *Ankylosaurus* to eat plants like ferns or even tougher species, as well as fleshy fruit. The lifestyle of this dinosaur, which is believed to have moved quite slowly, unless defending itself against predators, suggests that it needed to eat dozens of pounds of plants a day. In fact, *Ankylosaurus*'s broad ribcage, which unusual with its vertebral ribs fused to the vertebral column, held a very effective digestive system for managing the large quantity of plants it ate.

This illustration shows the reconstruction of the *Ankylosaurus* tail, as suggested by the "bilobed tail" theory. We still don't know whether the tail was used for defense, combat, or both

A MEDIEVAL TAIL

Ankylosaurus's tail looked like a medieval club because of the two osteoderms on the sides of the tip, which were much larger than all the others on its body. The size of the tail was impressive at more than 19 inches (49 cm) wide and over 24 inches (60 cm) long. But what was it used for? The skeletal structure of the tail suggests that it could be moved easily and quickly from side to side, and the last seven vertebrae were interlocked, making it stronger. This all suggests that it was used as a weapon, just like the club of a medieval knight in armor. The tail appears to have been so strong that it could even break the leg bones of the large predators that *Ankylosaurus* had to defend itself against.

ARGENTIN

DISTINCTIVE
FEATURES:
a massive body

OSAURUS

Its name means:
ARGENTINA LIZARD

WHERE IT LIVED:

South America

ITS WEIGHT:

55–110 tons
(50,000–100,000 kg)

ITS SIZE:

105–125 ft. (32–38 m) long

WHEN IT LIVED:

94 million years ago

| TRIASSIC | JURASSIC | CRETACEOUS |

Argentinosaurus is one of the largest dinosaurs to have ever walked on our planet. Only a few vertebrae, some leg bones, and fragments of its ribs have been found, but even from these few remains, it is possible to see just how huge this dinosaur was: the fibula (a bone in the lower part of the leg) was 5 feet (1.55 m) long, and one neck vertebra was 4.3 feet (1.3 m) wide. Paleontologists reconstructed *Argentinosaurus* by studying more complete skeletons of other similar dinosaurs. Its length was extraordinary, perhaps reaching 125 feet (38 m), and its shoulder height was 26 feet (8 m).

Its tail and neck were short compared to other sauropods, and its head was very small compared to the rest of the body, which must have been truly massive. *Argentinosaurus* probably lived in small herds that moved continuously in search of food, which consisted mainly of conifers (cone-bearing trees and shrubs).

THE DINOSAUR WALK

In 2013, a computer model of the skeleton and muscles of *Argentinosaurus* was created to study its speed and pace. Using a computer simulation, paleontologists were able to see this giant walking. The most efficient gait had the forelimbs and hind limbs on one side of the body moving simultaneously. As for its speed, the model achieved a top speed of just over 4.5 miles (7.2 km) per hour. This simulation showed that, despite its enormous size, *Argentinosaurus* was able to move easily and pretty fast.

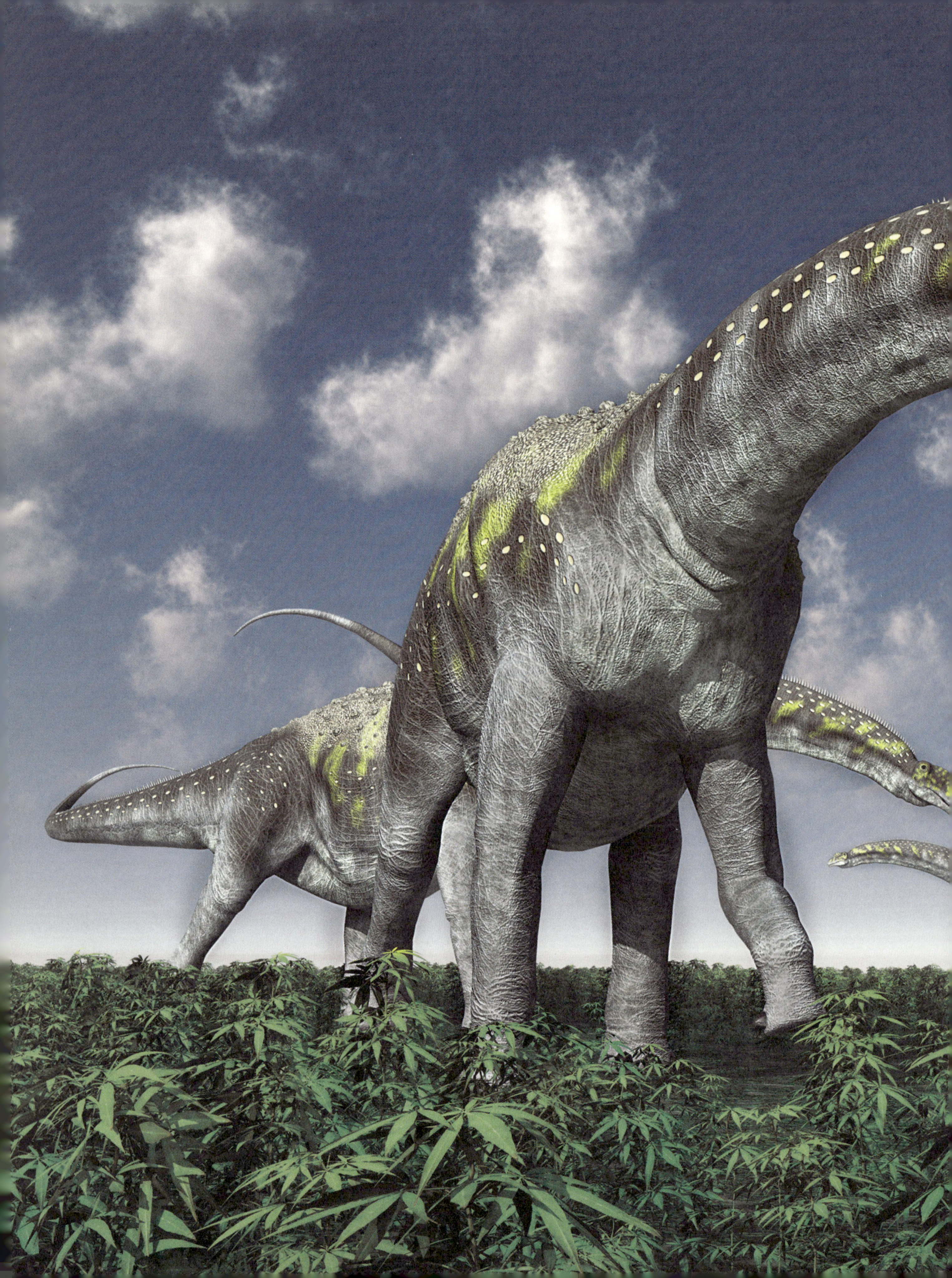

A small herd of *Argentinosaurus*

PARASAUR

Parasaurolophus was a plant eater, and like other similar dinosaurs, it was able to walk on either two or four legs. It probably preferred to stay on all fours when it moved in search of food, and it would use only its hind legs when it had to run. It would grind its food using a movement similar to chewing with hundreds of tiny teeth packed into groups called dental batteries in the back of its mouth. At the front of the mouth, however, it had a kind of beak that it used to crop plants from the ground, up to a height of about 13 feet (4 m).

Parasaurolophus's most distinctive feature, though, was the long, backward-curving crest atop its head. The crest was hollow and connected to the nose by internal tubes.

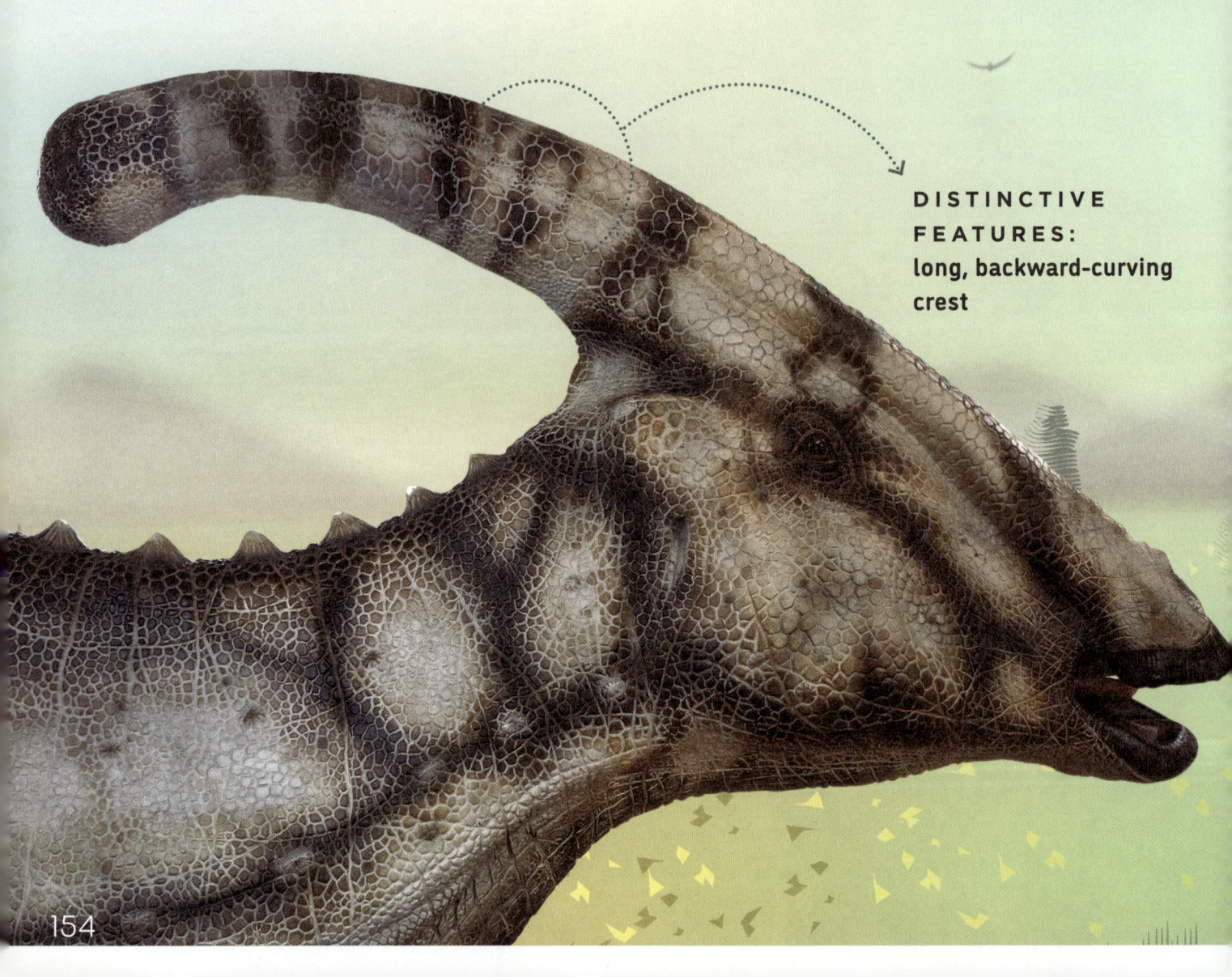

DISTINCTIVE FEATURES: long, backward-curving crest

...OLOPHUS

Its name means:
NEAR CRESTED LIZARD

WHERE IT LIVED:

North America

ITS WEIGHT:

2.8 tons (2,500 kg)

ITS SIZE:

31 ft. (9.5 m) long

WHEN IT LIVED:

76–73 million years ago

| TRIASSIC | JURASSIC | CRETACEOUS |

THE CREST DEBATE

Several hypotheses have been made about the purpose of *Parasaurolophus*'s crest. Some of these come from the belief that this dinosaur had a larger brain than other species as well as complex social behavior. So the crests likely were useful for recognizing each other as well as indicating the different ages or sex of the specimens. After analyzing the inside of the crest, paleontologists also think that low-frequency sounds were made inside the cavities and that the crests acted as an echo chamber to create warning signals or sounds for species recognition. This is supported by studies showing that their ears were also able to detect low-frequency sounds.

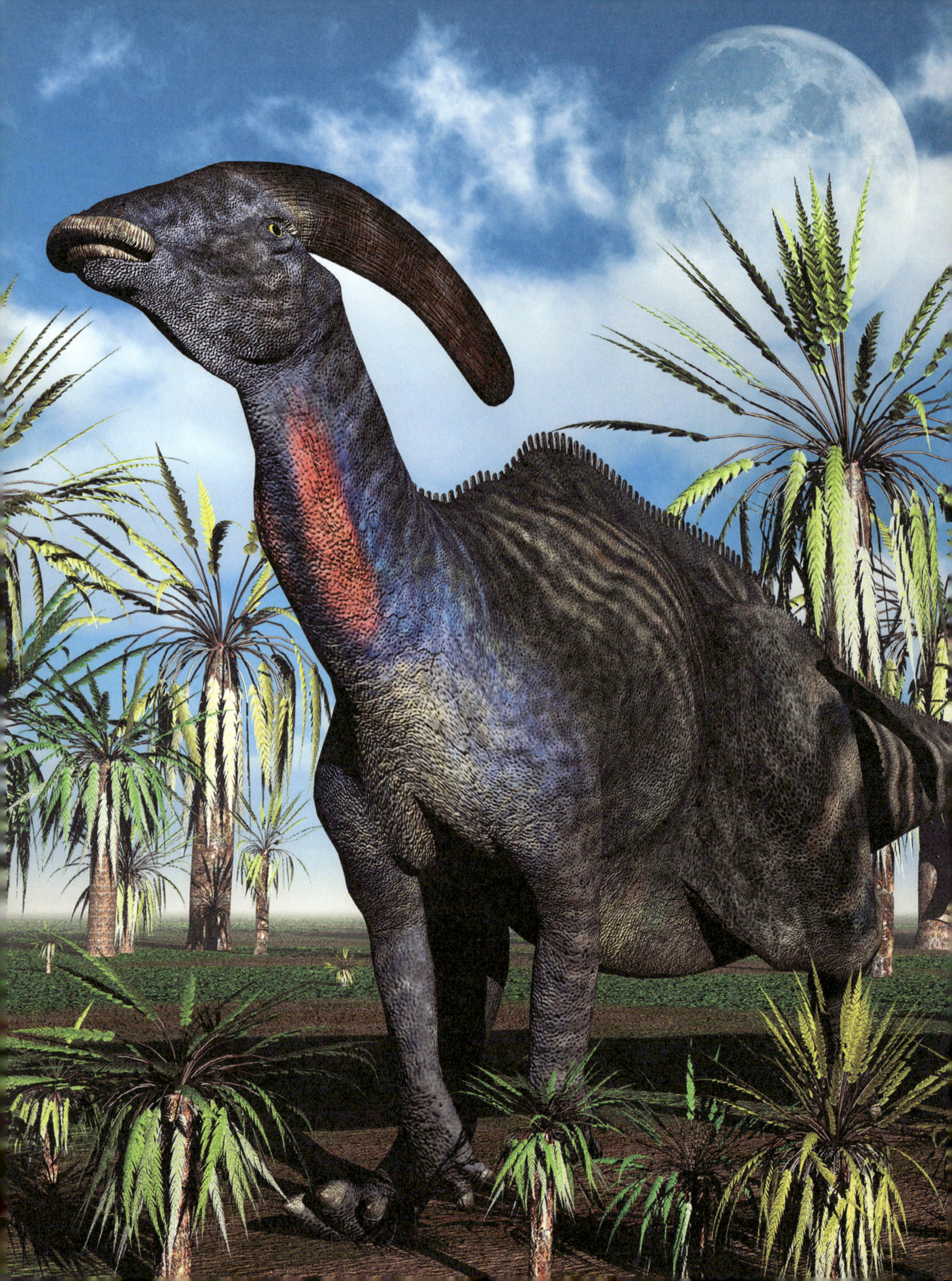

Two *Parasaurolophus* have noticed something moving behind them that put them on alert. This illustrates the moment before they start to run on two legs

OURANO

Ouranosaurus had a massive skeleton, with legs good for quadrupedal walking. However, the hind limbs, which had three sturdy toes, were strong enough for walking on them alone, but not running. So this dinosaur probably moved at a pretty slow pace. It had five fingers on each hand. The middle three were stronger and bore weight when *Ouranosaurus* was on four legs, and the "thumb" was like a spike.

The mouth had a kind of beak for tearing leaves off plants that grew on the edges of rivers and lakes, with a wide edge for collecting numerous plants at the same time. The teeth were at the back of the mouth and in two rows that formed a continuous surface. The presence of teeth suggests that *Ouranosaurus* probably also fed on the toughest parts of plants, like the stems and roots.

SAURUS

Its name means:
BRAVE LIZARD

WHERE IT LIVED:

Africa

ITS WEIGHT:

2.4 tons (2,200 kg)

ITS SIZE:

23–27 ft. (7–8.3 m) long

WHEN IT LIVED:

110–112 million years ago

| TRIASSIC | JURASSIC | CRETACEOUS |

DISTINCTIVE FEATURES:
very long back and tail vertebrae

Ouranosaurus's most impressive feature was the tall spines that grew out of the back and tail vertebrae, which would have supported either a skin-covered sail or a muscular hump. If Ouranosaurus had a sail, it may have served to regulate the dinosaur's body temperature, absorbing or releasing heat as needed. Another hypothesis is that the sail was used to attract mates and was a different color than the rest of the body. But if it had a hump, like bison do, the hump could have stored fat for survival when vegetation was scarce during long migrations in search of food, or when laying eggs.

AMARGA

There is only one known *Amargasaurus* skeleton. It was found in 1984 in Argentina, preserved in the rock formation called La Amarga, named after a nearby town. In addition to the skeleton being almost complete, the bones in the fossil were also in the correct anatomical position—that is, they were in exactly the same place as they were when the animal was alive. This made it easy to reconstruct its appearance! There were no doubts about the position of the spiny vertebrae that made *Amargasaurus* so unique.

DISTINCTIVE FEATURES: a double row of spines on its neck

SAURUS

Its name means:
AMARGA LIZARD

WHERE IT LIVED:

South America

ITS WEIGHT:

2.9 tons (2,600 kg)

ITS SIZE:

30–33 ft. (9–10 m) long

WHEN IT LIVED:

129–122 million years ago

TRIASSIC | JURASSIC | CRETACEOUS

These vertebrae, each with a **neural spine** split in two that could reach a length of up to 24 inches (60 cm), were still perfectly in line behind the skull, the front of which was not preserved. *Amargasaurus* is a small sauropod (of the same group as *Diplodocus* and other long-necked dinosaurs), with a short neck compared to that of other sauropods and a head similar to a horse's. Its teeth were likely the shape of a peg or pencil and used like rakes to strip the leaves it fed on from the branches. A study on its ear and the organ inside it that controlled balance provided some important information: *Amargasaurus* usually kept its head down, about 31.5 inches (80 cm) from the ground. This position could of course be changed when searching for food, but because of the spines and its inability to lift itself up on its hind legs, *Amargasaurus* could not feed on vegetation that was higher than 9 feet (2.7 m).

SPINES, SAIL, OR AIR POCKET?

As often happens when unusual structures are found in a fossil, several hypotheses have been made about the double row of spines on *Amargasaurus*'s neck. Some paleontologists suggested that they supported a pair of sails, similar to those of *Spinosaurus*, although this idea was rejected because it would have reduced the neck's flexibility. Other studies suggest that some of the spines contained an air sac made of skin, which would have been used like an extension of the lungs to increase **lung capacity.** There is also the theory that the spines were used as weapons to defend itself against predators or members of its own species. However, the spines curve backward, so the dinosaur would have been forced to bend its neck far back to use them. In 2019, *Bajadasaurus* was discovered, a dinosaur related to *Amargasaurus* which also has a similar double row of spines but curved forward, making the weapon theory much more likely. Of course, the spines may have been an ornament displayed during mating rituals, and there are those who think that the dinosaur could also rub them together by moving its neck in order to make a sound.

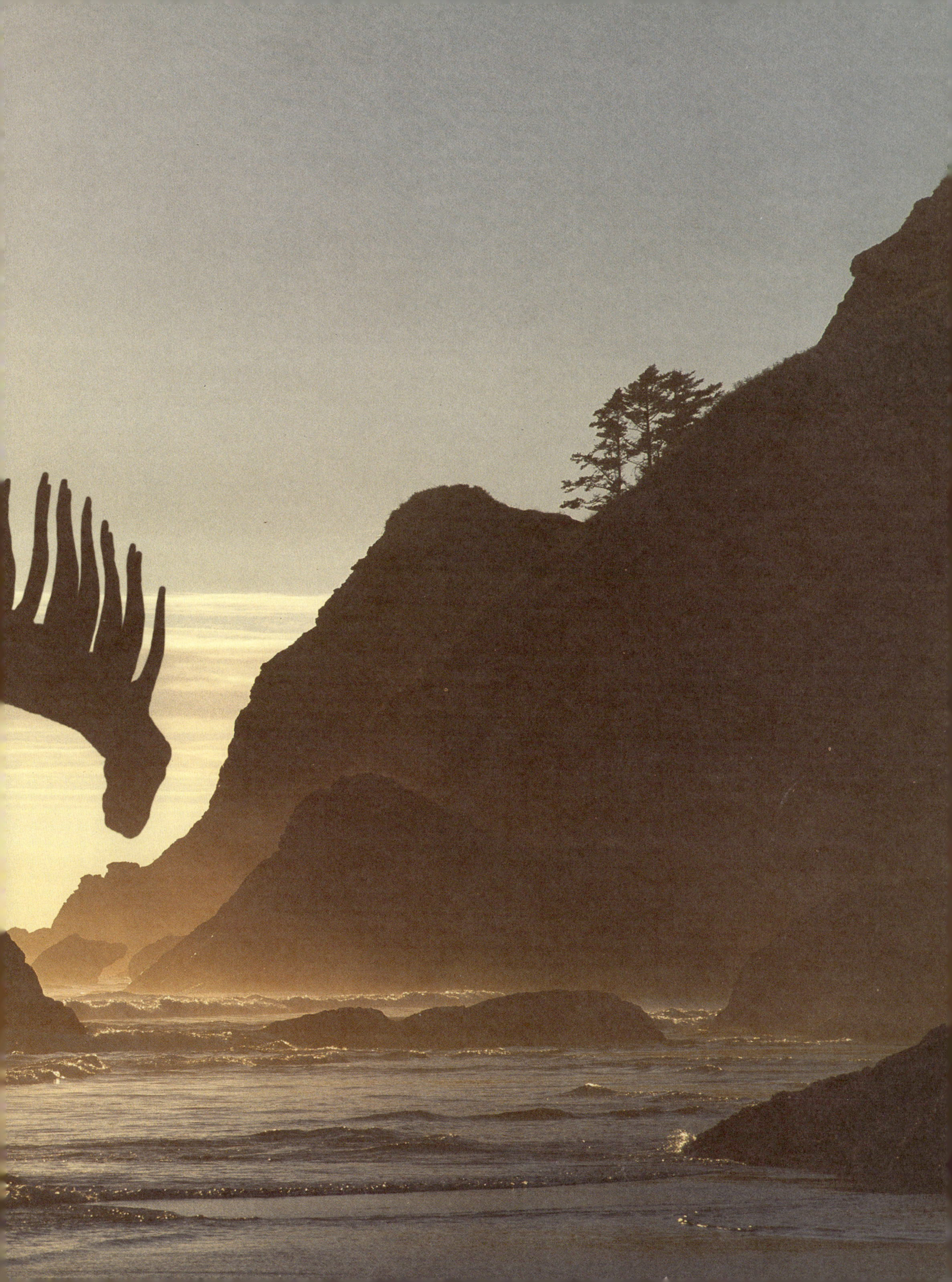

PLATEOS

Plateosaurus is a sauropodomorph dinosaur, which means "with the body form of a sauropod." It is considered an ancestor of the sauropods, which are large dinosaurs with a long neck.

Its gait has long been a mystery, but today most paleontologists agree that it was bipedal, with an almost horizontal back.

It had sharp teeth very similar to those of today's herbivorous reptiles both in the upper and lower jaw, and they overlapped like scissor blades for cutting plants but not grinding them.

Plateosaurus was therefore a herbivore, and its diet was based on conifers and ferns.

DISTINCTIVE FEATURES: a long neck and a small head

Thanks to its powerful tail, which it used to keep its balance, it could stand up on its hind limbs and then use its long neck to reach the leaves on even the tallest trees.

Each hand had four very flexible fingers and a powerful clawed thumb useful for grabbing branches and collecting food from trees and for defending itself against predators.

More than fifty *Plateosaurus* skeletons have been found, mostly in Germany but some in Greenland and other areas.

AURUS

Its name means:
BROAD LIZARD

WHERE IT LIVED:

Greenland
Europe

ITS WEIGHT:

1.3–8 tons (600–4,000 kg)

ITS SIZE:

16–33 ft. (4.8–10 m)

WHEN IT LIVED:

214–204 million years ago

| TRIASSIC | JURASSIC | CRETACEOUS |

A BONE AT THE BOTTOM OF THE SEA

An odd discovery was made in 1997 while drilling for oil off the coast of Norway: a fossil was found in a cylinder of rock that was pulled from an incredible 1.6 miles (2,615 m) below the seabed. At first it was mistaken for a plant. A later study showed that it was a section of a long bone from *Plateosaurus*, making it the first dinosaur ever found in Norway.

LAMBEO

DISTINCTIVE FEATURES: a very tall crest on its head

Lambeosaurus was primarily quadrupedal, but it could walk on only its hind legs when necessary. This meant it could feed on plants both on the ground and high up. After the food passed through the front of the mouth, which had a duck-like beak, it was shredded by tight rows of teeth, called dental batteries, in the back.

However, *Lambeosaurus*'s most distinctive feature was its crest, which is often described as resembling a hatchet, or ax. The wider "blade" was at the front, and the thin "handle" jutted out over the back of the skull. The back part was solid, while the front part was hollow with a network of tubes inside.

SAURUS

Its name means:
LAMBE'S LIZARD

WHERE IT LIVED:

North America

ITS WEIGHT:

3 tons (3,000 kg)

ITS SIZE:

up to 31 ft. (9.5 m) long

WHEN IT LIVED:

75 million years ago

| TRIASSIC | JURASSIC | CRETACEOUS |

MANY HYPOTHESES FOR JUST ONE CREST

The striking structures found in fossils always attract the attention of paleontologists. But understanding their function isn't always easy and sometimes bizarre theories are suggested. *Lambeosaurus*'s crest is no exception. One of the first hypotheses was that the crest may have stored salt glands, which are special organs that remove extra salt from the body. Other theories suggested that the crest improved the sense of smell served as an air storage chamber. Today, however, it is believed that —like *Parasaurolophus*— the crest was mainly used for species recognition.

The various species of *Lambeosaurus* would have been able to identify each other based on the different shapes of these crests. Also, the crests of *Lambeosaurus* adults were more developed than those of juveniles, which indicates that crests were also a sign of maturity. The female specimens have more rounded crests than males.

Last, the hollow part of the crest, with a network of tubes, could have formed an echo chamber to amplify the dinosaur's calls.

THERIZIN

Therizinosaurus's most distinctive features were the long claws on the three fingers on its hands. They were the longest claws of any other known land animal.

The claws were the first remains of *Therizinosaurus* to be found in the Gobi Desert in Mongolia, in 1948. Although only a few parts of its skeleton have been found, and at first it was mistaken for a turtle, its appearance was reconstructed by comparing it with

OSAURUS

Its name means:
SCYTHE LIZARD

WHERE IT LIVED:

Asia

ITS WEIGHT:

3–5 tons
(2,700–4,500 kg)

ITS SIZE:

30–33 ft. (9–10 m) long

other therizinosaurs. It was bipedal with four toes on its hind feet, making it a slow-moving dinosaur, and it had a long neck, a skull with a beak, and a large abdomen for digesting plants. It was also feathered, mainly on the forelimbs. It appears to have been the largest member of its group. Indeed, it was so large that not even its main predator, the tyrannosaurid dinosaur *Tarbosaurus*, would have been able to bite it any higher than its belly.

WHEN IT LIVED:

70 million years ago

| TRIASSIC | JURASSIC | CRETACEOUS |

DISTINCTIVE FEATURES:
gigantic hand claws

HERBIVORE CLAWS

Therizinosaurus's claws were over 1.6 feet (0.5 m) long and were much straighter than the curved claws of other therizinosaurs. Their function is still being studied today. There is no evidence to support or disprove that they were used as a defensive weapon against predators or in combat with individuals of the same species. Also, the claws may have been used to hold down a partner during mating. However, the most convincing theory seems to be that they were mainly used to pull up vegetation and then to put it in their mouths.

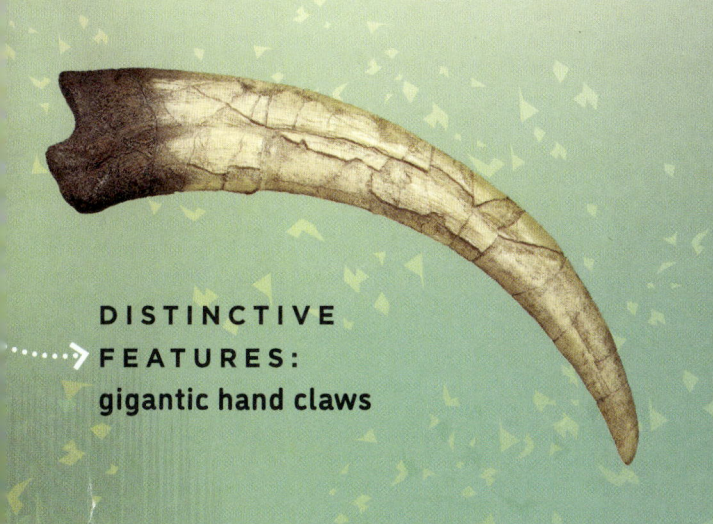

STEGOS

This dinosaur owes its name to Othniel Charles Marsh, the paleontologist who discovered it during the "Bone Wars," when between 1877 and 1892 the rivalry between Marsh and Edward Drinker Cope led to the discovery of more than 130 new dinosaur species. When Marsh unearthed the first *Stegosaurus* bones and saw the plates, he thought that they laid flat on the dinosaur's back, like tiles on a roof. Today, paleontologists agree that the plates were arranged vertically in two staggered rows. Starting from the neck, they gradually increased in size to the pelvis, reaching a height of 24 inches (60 cm), and then they got smaller as they went down the tail, where they were replaced by two pairs of spikes.

DISTINCTIVE FEATURES: large plates on its back

...AURUS

Its name means:
ROOF LIZARD

WHERE IT LIVED:

North America
Europe

ITS WEIGHT:

5–7 tons (4,500–6,300 kg)

ITS SIZE:

30 ft. (9 m) long

WHEN IT LIVED:

155–150 million years ago

TRIASSIC | JURASSIC | CRETACEOUS

Stegosaurus was quadrupedal, and due to its front legs being much shorter than the back legs, its posture was rather odd. It kept its head low to the ground, and its tail high in the air. The different lengths of its limbs suggest that its maximum speed was less than 3.7–4.3 miles per hour (6–7 km/h). Even at this speed, the stride of the back legs would have overtaken the front legs, and this kind of movement is unlikely.

Stegosaurus also had an unusual skull. It was very small compared to the body, and about one-third of the length of the mouth was a toothless, beak-like structure. In the back two-thirds of the mouth were small, serrated, triangular teeth. Signs of wear have been found on the teeth, suggesting that it was able to chew vegetation. For a long time, these dinosaurs were considered unintelligent animals due to their very small brain. This led to the popular myth that Stegosauruses had a second brain in their sacral cavity (where the spine met the pelvis) that functioned as the operating center for the back half of the dinosaur. Today, we know this is not true.

THE PLATES

In addition to doubts about their position, there has been much debate about the function of *Stegosaurus*'s plates. Studies on these structures revealed that they contained many blood vessels and were covered with keratin (the substance our nails are made of). This means the plates grew quickly, and the covering probably also made them sharp and colorful. The *Stegosaurus* shared its habitat with large carnivores, such as *Allosauruses*, and the plates could have been used both as a defensive weapon and as a way to look bigger to its enemies. However, they may also have been used for species recognition and displayed during mating rituals.

THE THAGOMIZER

The *Stegosaurus* had two pairs of spikes extending about 3.3 feet (1 m) horizontally near the end of its tail. The flexibility of the tail and the dinosaur's ability to push off with its forelimbs to "pivot" on its hind legs made this structure of spikes—now known as a thagomizer—a truly effective weapon. This hypothesis is supported by numerous injuries found on the spines and one vertebra of an *Allosaurus*, along with a hole that is a perfect match to a *Stegosaurus*'s tail spike.

There is a unique story that led to the naming of this part of the *Stegosaurus*'s body. The arrangement of spikes originally had no official name. In 1982, cartoonist Gary Larson invented the name "thagomizer" as a joke in his comic strip *The Far Side*, and it was eventually adopted as an informal term used within scientific circles.

ALTIRHI

Unlike many similar dinosaurs, *Altirhinus* was mostly bipedal when it walked or ran. Its front limbs were about one-half the length of its hind limbs, but it had massive wrist bones, and the three middle fingers on each hand were broad and ended in hoof-like structures. This indicates that its arms were able to support the dinosaur's weight, so it could stand on all four legs when necessary, such as when feeding on plants low to the ground. Its "thumb" had a strong spike that it used as a defensive weapon or to break shells and seeds.

NUS

Its name means:
HIGH NOSE

WHERE IT LIVED:

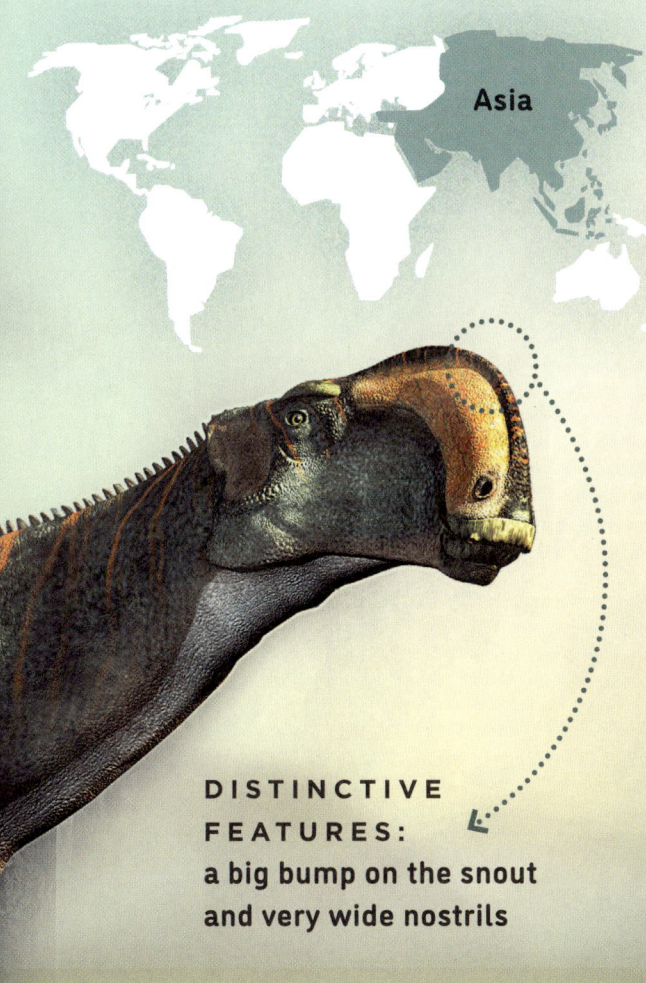

Asia

ITS WEIGHT:

1.1 tons (1,000 kg)

ITS SIZE:

21 ft. (6.5 m) long

WHEN IT LIVED:

110 million years ago

| TRIASSIC | JURASSIC | CRETACEOUS |

DISTINCTIVE FEATURES:
a big bump on the snout and very wide nostrils

Altirhinus's mouth had a large, empty space between the beak in the front and the teeth in the back. This would have allowed the dinosaur to crop vegetation with its beak and chew with its teeth at the same time.

A HIGH NOSE

One of *Altirhinus*'s most striking features is the big arched bump on the end of its snout. Paleontologists think it may have contained special structures that could regulate the body temperature by cooling the incoming air or improve the dinosaur's sense of smell. Another hypothesis is that only males had this bump and that it was used for display or to make certain sounds.

IGUANOD

Iguanodon was one of the first dinosaurs to be discovered in the Ceratopsidae family in the 1820s, before the name *dinosaur* was even coined. Legend has it that Mary Ann Mantell found the first fossils, which were some teeth, while her husband, Dr. Gideon Mantell, was visiting a patient, although a few years later he claimed to have made the discovery. Dr. Mantell was immediately intrigued by the teeth.

He had already been fascinated by the discovery of some large bones a few years earlier, which he had then bought to study. According to him, the teeth must have belonged to a large, extinct, herbivorous reptile. Although respected scientists such as the French naturalist Georges Cuvier were doubtful at first, Mantell continued with his studies. He discovered that the teeth were very similar to those of iguanas, which feed on plants, confirming his hypotheses. He estimated that their owner was about 40 feet (12 m) long. However, the first reconstructions of *Iguanodon* were wrong, showing it as a lizard with an odd horn on its nose.

DISTINCTIVE FEATURES:
a large thumb spike

Its name means:
IGUANA TOOTH

WHERE IT LIVED:

Europe

ITS WEIGHT:

3–4 tons (2,700–3,600 kg)

ITS SIZE:

33–43 ft. (10–13 m) long

WHEN IT LIVED:

126–122 million years ago

TRIASSIC | JURASSIC | CRETACEOUS

An Iguanodon's tooth

Later findings showed that the horn was actually the tip of a thumb that had transformed into a large, straight spike shaped like a pyramid. Over the years, *Iguanodon*'s entire appearance has undergone many changes, and today it is shown in a quadrupedal position, although it could stand up on its hind legs if necessary.

Its head was large, and it had a rounded, toothless beak. There were about sixty teeth in the back of the mouth, arranged in a single row. The tail was straight and stiff due to ossified tendons (fibrous structures that change into bone over time). It had three toes on its hind feet and five fingers on each hand.

Many individuals were found together at a fossil site in a coal mine in Belgium, suggesting that *Iguanodons* traveled in herds. This group of dinosaurs appears to have died together during a flood. However, the main victims in this type of disaster, which affects numerous herds, are usually juveniles, and there were hardly any at this site.

HANDS WITH MANY FUNCTIONS

In addition to the thumb spike, it had three middle fingers that ended in a bone that had a shape similar to a hoof, and a very flexible fifth finger (the little finger). Today, *Iguanodon*'s hand is reconstructed as a fleshy hoof composed of the three middle fingers, which supported the weight of the animal, and the thumb and the little finger sticking out to the side. The flexible, prehensile, or grasping, fifth finger would have made it easier for *Iguanodon* to grab the branches it fed on as it stood up on its hind legs. The function of its big thumb spike, however, is still debated. Was it used for stabbing attackers or as a tool for stripping foliage from branches? Perhaps discoveries in the future will provide the answer.

MYSTERIOUS FOOTPRINTS

In the first half of the 19th century, a series of footprints was found on the Isle of Wight in England in which the marks left by three clawless digits were clearly visible. The identity of the animal that had left them remained a mystery until 1857, when the hind leg of an *Iguanodon* was found. While it had five fingers on each of its hands, it only had three toes on its feet, each with a large rounded nail.

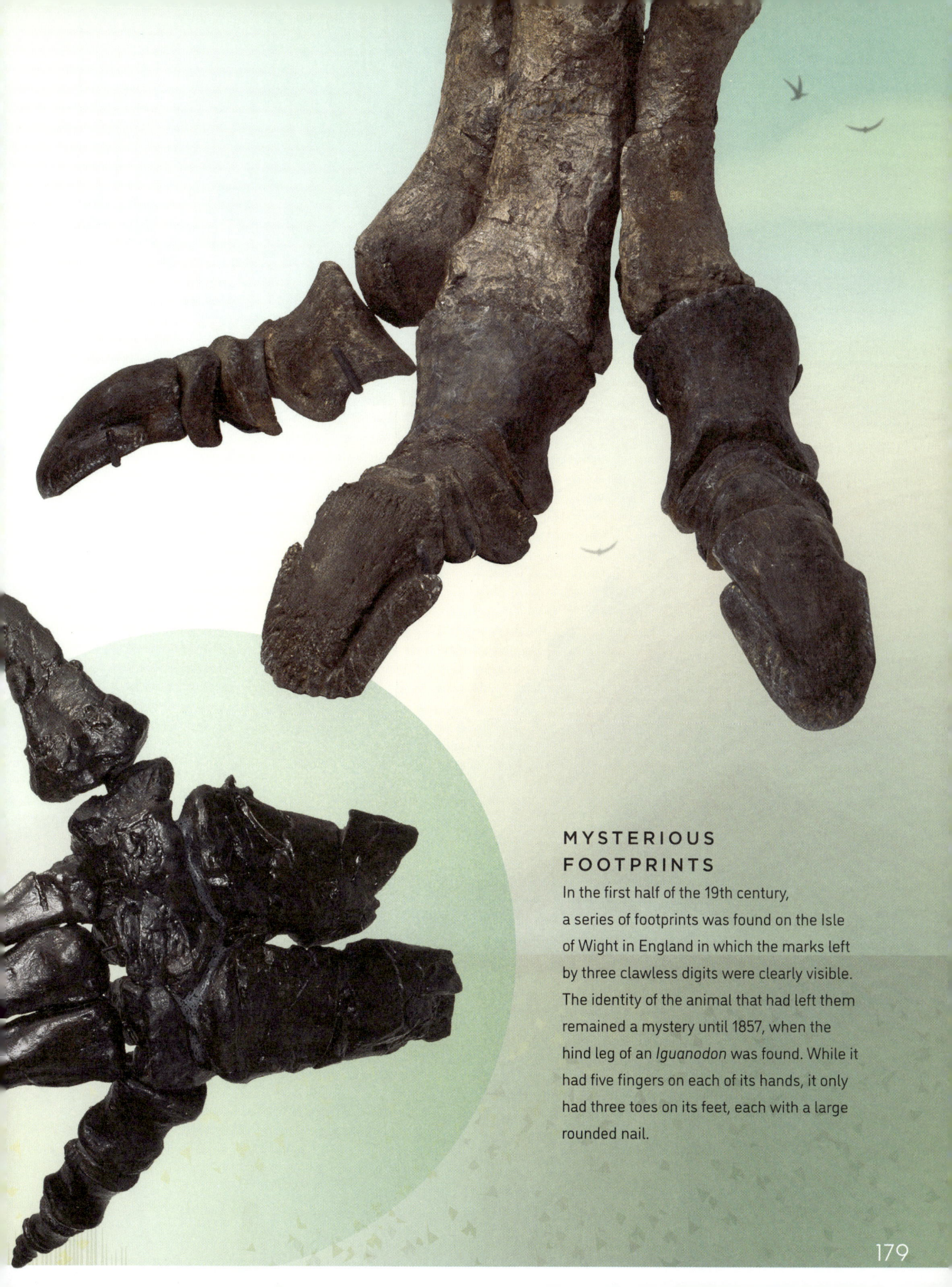

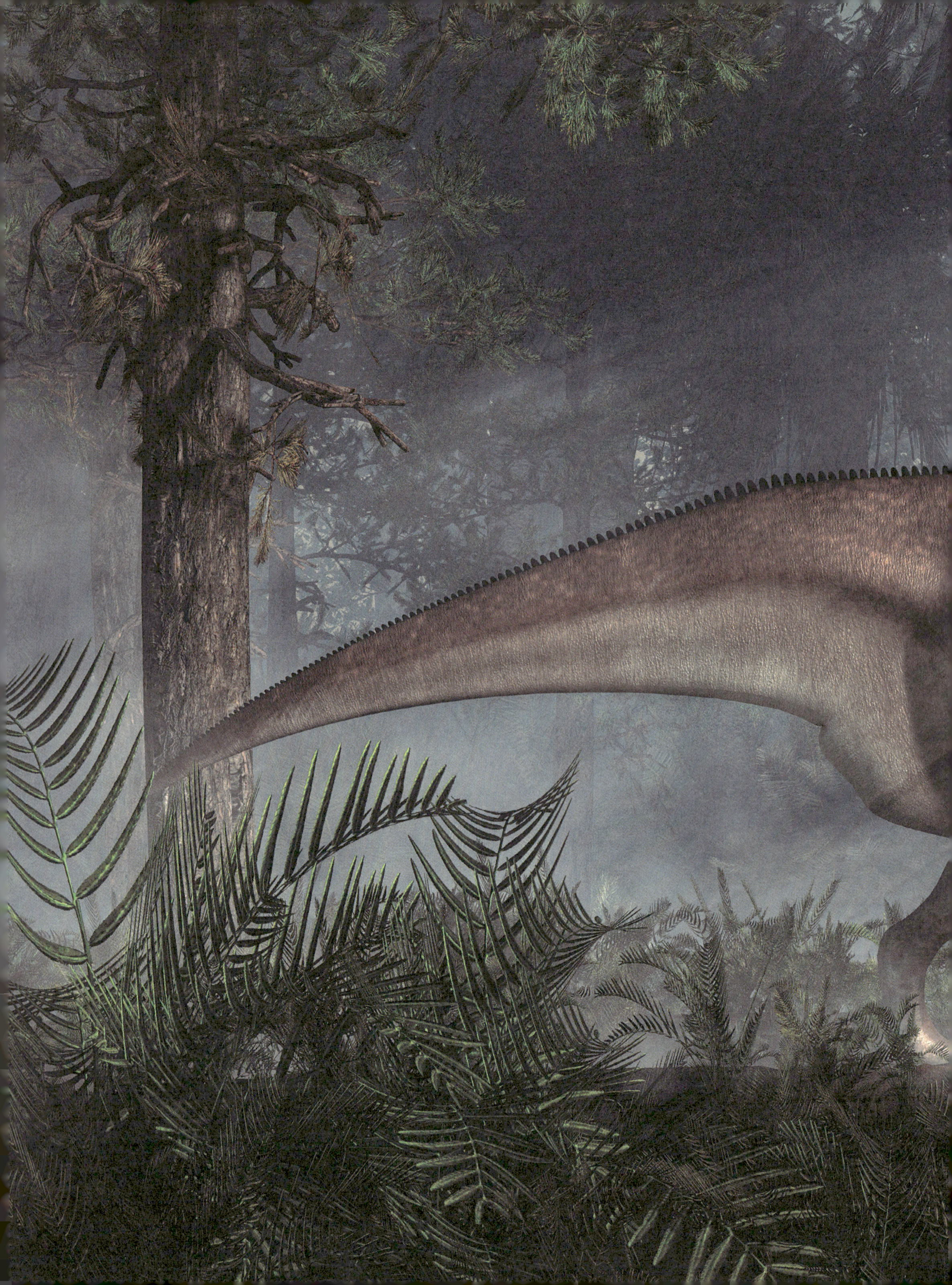

An *Iguanodon* in its ideal habitat

PTEROS

While dinosaurs ruled the earth, another group of reptiles, the pterosaurs, were the kings of the sky and remained so until the end of the Mesozoic era.

The first pterosaurs were relatively small and had long, bony tails, which on later specimens were either much smaller or absent. Some of these later species reached gigantic sizes, about the size of a small airplane!

Their wings were modified forelimbs, and the extremely long fourth finger supported a membrane of skin, the **patagium**, whose wide surface area equipped these animals for **gliding**. Species with very long, narrow wings could fly continuously for months, like albatrosses, only landing on the ground to mate or lay eggs. The bones of pterosaurs were hollow, making them incredibly lightweight, and were just a few millimeters thick. Larger species had thin struts inside the wing bones, which strengthened them without adding any weight. Unlike birds, pterosaurs also used their massive wings for quadrupedal walking and jumping. Many pterosaurs had a head that was much larger than their body, making their jaws a lethal weapon. In the late Jurassic, the head of *Rhamphorynchus* was almost as long as its body.

Pterosaurs were Earth's first flying vertebrates. They filled the skies millions of years before birds and bats and spread across all the continents, diversifying over time, for over 140 million years

A *Pteranodon*, flying

AURS

> The name means
> **FLYING REPTILES**

During the next period, the Cretaceous, the heads of the pterosaurs got bigger and bigger, with some becoming four times longer than their bodies. The parts that developed the most were the expansions on the jawbone and the immense head crests, while the skull itself remained small. Despite this, they had a highly specialized brain, particularly the cerebellum, which was responsible for wing movements.

How did pterosaurs reproduce? This is not yet clear. Some information has been gained from a *Darwinopterus* fossil dating back to 160 million years ago that was found in the Chinese province of Liaoning. The specimen is a fossilized mother and her egg, which was pushed out of her body after her death. Chemical analysis of the egg suggests that the shell was soft and had tiny holes. This suggests that pterosaurs, unlike birds, buried their eggs in moist ground, and that the young could take care of themselves from birth.

QUETZAL

Quetzalcoatlus was a flying reptile with long legs and a pair of wings that were short compared with its body. The most notable thing about this reptile is the immense size it could reach, making it the largest **pterosaur** ever found. It had a very long, sharp, toothless beak and a crest on the back of its head, the exact size and shape of which are still unknown.

DISTINCTIVE FEATURES: its huge size

LAND OR SEA PREDATORS?

Quetzalcoatluses were certainly predators, but paleontologists have disagreed about how they hunted their prey. At first, paleontologists thought that they skimmed the water's surface with their long lower bill to catch fish.

COATLUS

Its name means:
THE FEATHERED SERPENT (AFTER THE AZTEC GOD QUETZACOATL)

WHERE IT LIVED:

North America

ITS WEIGHT:

440–551 lb. (200–250 kg)

ITS SIZE:

33–36-ft. (10–11-m) wingspan

WHEN IT LIVED:

68–66 million years ago

TRIASSIC	JURASSIC	CRETACEOUS

Later research shows that its large size wouldn't have worked with this fishing technique. Also, the front and hind limbs suggest that these flying reptiles may have been better suited to walking on land than we would have expected. *Quetzacoatlus* may have eaten like storks do today, walking like quadrupeds and swallowing anything they could fit into their mouths, including small dinosaurs.

This *Quetzalcoatlus*, which is carnivorous, is looking for its prey hidden in the vegetation

THE POWER TO FLY

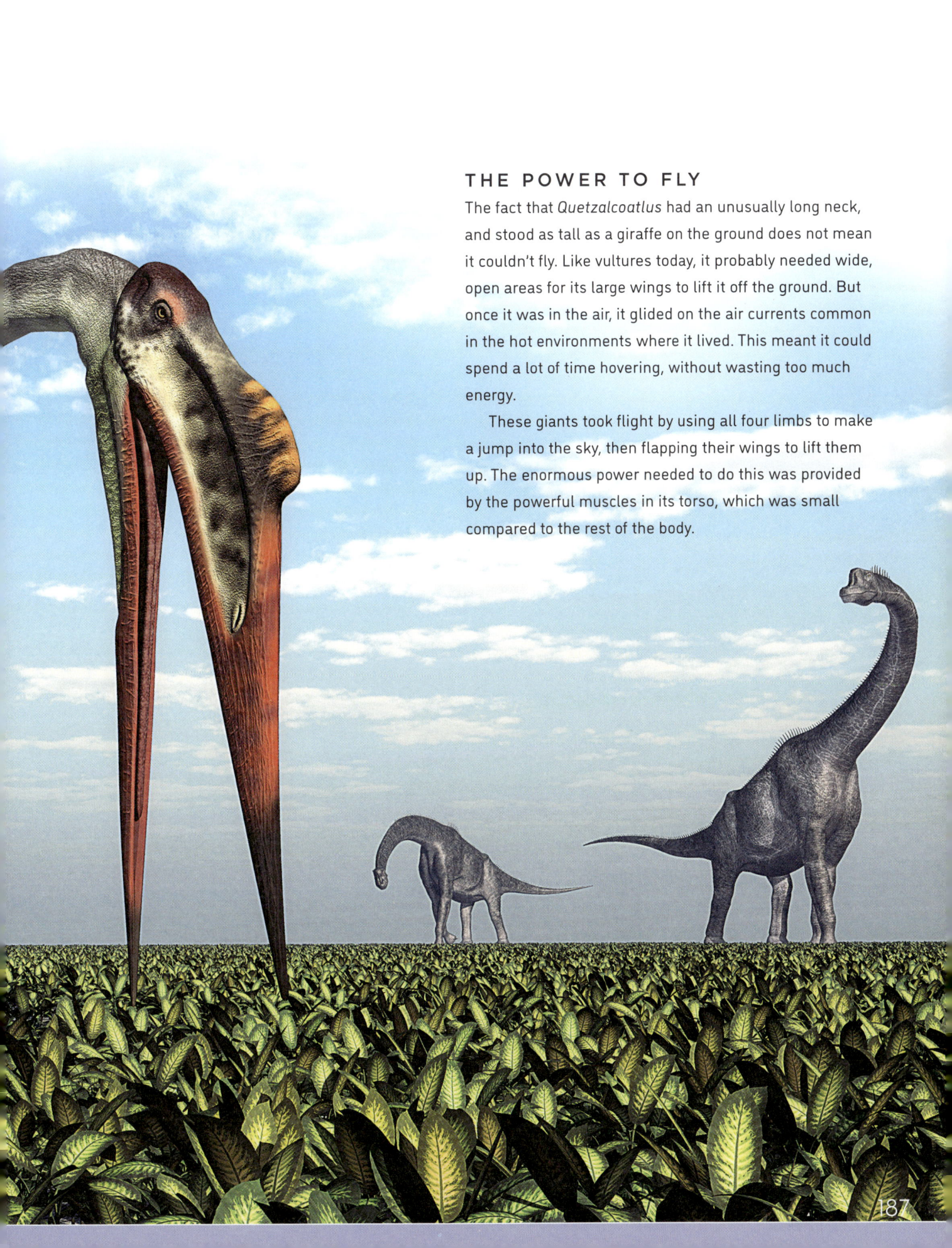

The fact that *Quetzalcoatlus* had an unusually long neck, and stood as tall as a giraffe on the ground does not mean it couldn't fly. Like vultures today, it probably needed wide, open areas for its large wings to lift it off the ground. But once it was in the air, it glided on the air currents common in the hot environments where it lived. This meant it could spend a lot of time hovering, without wasting too much energy.

These giants took flight by using all four limbs to make a jump into the sky, then flapping their wings to lift them up. The enormous power needed to do this was provided by the powerful muscles in its torso, which was small compared to the rest of the body.

PTERAN

Pteranodon was a large flying reptile that was very widespread during the Cretaceous era. About 1,200 partial skeletons of this genus have been found, more than those of any other pterosaur. **Pycnofibers** on the head and body of many pterosaurs probably had a function similar to hairs in mammals: to keep the body temperature of these animals constant. Its body was stocky compared to the size of the wings, and it didn't have a tail. The hind limbs, on the other hand, were large compared with the torso. However, its most distinctive feature was its head: the skull was enormous, and there was a long crest growing out of the back. The crest may have been used for species recognition and, because the male's crest was larger, displays during mating. Perhaps the crest helped balance the weight of the jaws or was necessary for steering in flight. Female *Pteranodons*, which were half the size of the males, had only a small bump.

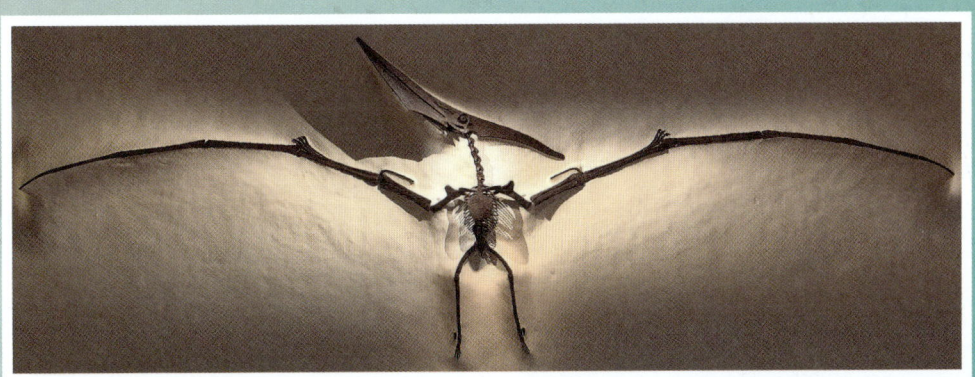

ODON

Its name means:
WINGED AND TOOTHLESS

WHERE IT LIVED:

North America

DISTINCTIVE FEATURES:
a long, toothless beak

ITS WEIGHT:

44 lb. (20 kg)

ITS SIZE:

120–123-ft. (6–7-m) wingspan

WHEN IT LIVED:

85 million years ago

| TRIASSIC | JURASSIC | CRETACEOUS |

A FLYING MACHINE

In addition to the large wings made of skin, which stretched between the fourth finger and the body, many more parts confirm that *Pteranodon*, like many other pterosaurs, was an excellent flier: a large **sternum**, sturdy shoulder joints, muscular attachments on the very large arm bones, and its light bones. These bones were no more than 0.04 inches (1 mm) thick, and their shape made them very resistant to **aerodynamic forces** of flight. The hollow bones meant that *Pteranodon* had a highly effective breathing system. In fact, tissue from the lungs extended into these bones, as in birds today. This system would also help to cool the blood from the efforts of flight.

Its large size probably prevented the animal from flapping its wings for prolonged lengths of time, so it was primarily a glider. Like today's albatrosses, this large pterosaur probably spent much of its time flying over the ocean, rarely returning to land and mainly to breed. Since numerous *Pteranodon* fossils have been found in locations that would have been hundreds of miles from the coastline, *Pteranodon* likely got its food from the sea.

STORING MEALS FOR LATER OR EATING ON THE SPOT

The discovery of fossil fish bones and scales in the stomach area of one specimen suggests that this animal was a fish eater. The large, toothless beak would have been used to trap prey that it spotted from above, depending on sight thanks to its large eyes. The fragments of fish scales and vertebrae near the torso, however, suggest that it had a pouch of skin under its beak, similar to that of pelicans. Recent studies show that despite their size, these pterosaurs were also able to dive directly into the sea, with their wings folded close to the body like pelicans.

When flying over the ocean in search of fish, a *Pteranodon* could encounter unexpected predators

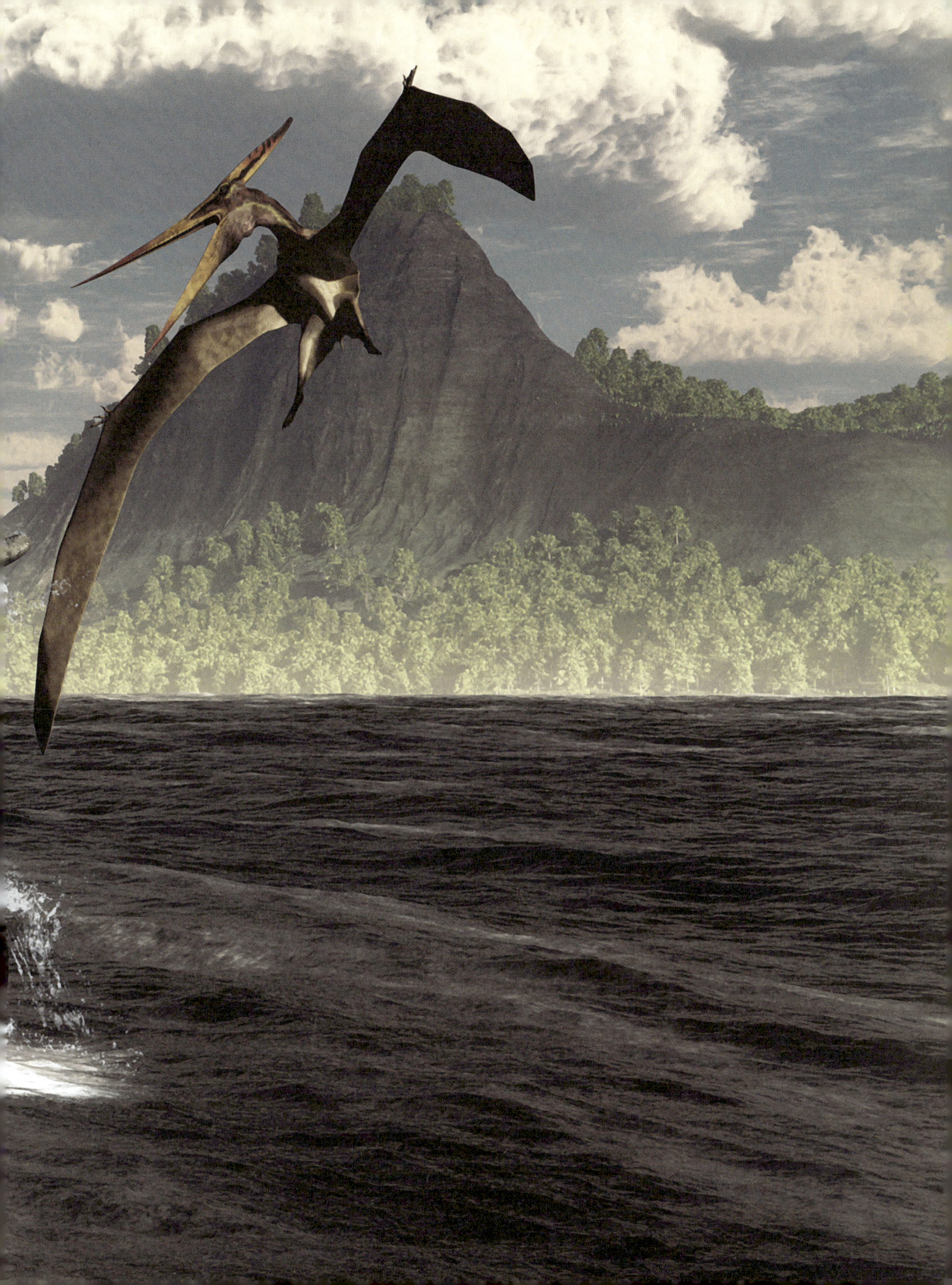

PTERODA

Pterodactylus was one of the first flying reptiles discovered at the end of the 18th century. Italian scientist Cosimo Collini wrote the first description of the fossil found in the Solnhofen Limestone formation in Germany. Unfortunately, he mistakenly assumed that the wings were flippers for swimming, and he described it as a marine animal. It was the German scientist Johann Hermann who realized that the fourth finger on the hand must have supported a membrane that formed a wing very similar to that of bats. The great French anatomist Georges Cuvier then gave it an appropriate name.

DISTINCTIVE FEATURES: a long beak with 90 teet

CTYLUS

Its name means:
WINGED FINGER

WHERE IT LIVED:

Europe

ITS WEIGHT:

up to 10 lb. (4.5 kg)

ITS SIZE:

3.3-ft. (1-m) wingspan

WHEN IT LIVED:

150 million years ago

| TRIASSIC | JURASSIC | CRETACEOUS |

ACTIVE DURING THE DAY

Studies on sclerotic rings, which are bony structures surrounding the eyeballs, show that *Pterodactylus* searched for food during daylight hours. Due to the shape and size of its teeth, its habits and lifestyle were very likely similar to those of today's seabirds. It likely got its food from the sea by mainly catching small invertebrates and fish with its long snout.

THE CREST

The discovery of imprints of skin and **collagen** fibers and remains of muscle fibers have led to new reconstructions of this animal. The hypothesis that *Pterodactylus* had a small, smooth, thin crest on its head, made up of soft tissue, is also recent. The size of the crest varied by age and was only fully developed in adults.

RHAMPHOR

We owe our knowledge of *Rhamphorhynchus* to the discovery of incredibly well-preserved specimens in the Solnhofen fossil deposit in Germany. These fossils show not only the bone structure but also the imprints of internal organs and wing membranes, including the flap of skin at the end of the tail.

This has made it possible to confirm that these pterosaurs did not have any type of crest on their heads. Studies show that although it probably obtained similar food as *Pterodactylus*, it was active mostly at night.

DISTINCTIVE FEATURES: a long tail with a flap of skin at the end

HYNCHUS

Its name means: BEAK SNOUT

WHERE IT LIVED:

Europe
Africa

ITS WEIGHT:

4.4 lb. (2 kg)

ITS SIZE:

3.3-ft. (1-m) wingspan

WHEN IT LIVED:

150 million years ago

| TRIASSIC | JURASSIC | CRETACEOUS |

PREDATOR OR PREY?

Its mouth was filled with long, pointed teeth, suggesting that *Rhamphorhynchus* was **piscivorous**, or fish eating. The mouth functioned like a trap to grab fast-moving prey just below the surface of the water.

Proof of this is a specimen containing the remains of a *Leptolepides*, a small fish similar to a herring. The *Rhamphorhynchus* then fell prey to an *Aspidorhynchus*, a large and fast predatory fish with the size and appearance of a pike. The fibrous tissue of the *Rhamphorhynchus*'s wing membrane got caught between the *Aspidorhynchus*'s teeth, and the fish wasn't able to free itself of the indigestible prey. They both died in the struggle and sank to the bottom of the sea, destined for fossilization.

SMALL PTEROSAURS GROW FAST

There are many juveniles among the *Rhamphorhynchus* specimens that have been found. By studying their fossil remains, paleontologists have figured out their growth pattern, which appears rather unusual. As soon as they were born, the hatchlings started growing very fast, reaching half the size of an adult in a very short time. They did not depend on their parents for food, but they may not have been able to fly well enough to hunt for food either.

They probably led a mostly **arboreal** life, climbing trees like young hoatzins (South American birds whose chicks have two claws on each wing) and feeding on small **arthropods** and insects. They would start flying only when they were half the size of the adults, catching different types of prey in the water. They developed fully during the second growth stage, which was slower than the first.

TAPEJAR[A]

The most distinctive feature of *Tapejara* was the crest on its head, which was a thin, bony plate that extended upward from its small eye sockets. The crest probably worked like a rudder, allowing it to cut through the air and improving flight. The crest may have been brightly colored on males and used to recognize others and attract females during the mating season.

DISTINCTIVE FEATURES: the structure on the underside of the jaw

DISTINCTIVE FEATURES: a rounded crest on its snout

Its name means:
THE OLD BEING

WHERE IT LIVED:

South America

ITS WEIGHT:

less than 2.2 lb. (1 kg)

ITS SIZE:

4.6-ft. (1.4-m) wingspan

A FRUIT DIET

The very short, toothless beak may have been useful for picking fruit and berries because, unlike most meat-eating pterosaurs, the small *Tapejara* was probably **frugivorous**. In fact, its beak—strong and good for crushing seeds, pine cones, and nutshells—was very similar to that of today's fruit-eating birds, such as parrots and hornbills.

WHEN IT LIVED:

112 million years ago

| TRIASSIC | JURASSIC | CRETACEOUS |

ON LAND AND IN THE AIR

Although it had wings, *Tapejara* was also agile on land. It walked by folding its wings back and putting its hands on the ground, which also allowed it to run for short bursts. To fly, it probably launched itself from a high point, gaining height with a few powerful wing strokes. *Tapejara* never strayed too far from the coast.

TUPANDA

The crest on this flying reptile's head must have made it look pretty strange, and it was so large that paleontologists can't imagine how it was able to fly or even hold up or move its head. The fossils also show the presence of keratin, which probably made this structure even bigger. The species *Tupandactylus imperator*, shown on page 203, also had a long, bony prong that extended backward from the head and a smaller crest on the underside of the jaw, like a keel on a boat.

DISTINCTIVE FEATURES: the largest crest of any known flying reptile

...CTYLUS

Its name means:
FINGER OF THE TUPI GOD

WHERE IT LIVED:

South America

ITS WEIGHT:

110–132 lb. (50–60 kg)

ITS SIZE:

16.4-ft. (5-m) wingspan

WHEN IT LIVED:

112 million years ago

| TRIASSIC | JURASSIC | CRETACEOUS |

STAYING WARM

Like many other pterosaurs, *Tupandactylus*'s entire body, including its jaws, was covered in hair-like filaments known as pycnofibers. There were two types of pycnofibers: one was longer (up to 1.6 inches/4 cm), thinner, and lighter in color, and the other was thicker, shorter (less than 0.4 inches/1 cm), and darker. The pycnofibers probably served to conserve heat, like fur, and perhaps also for display during mating.

TODAY'S MENU

Tupandactylus fossils are often found near **lacustrine** (lake) environments. Therefore this pterosaur probably ate a fish-based diet, although more recent scientific research on the shape of its toothless jaw suggests that the animal may have enjoyed a wider variety of foods, including fruit and seeds as well as small vertebrates, making it an omnivore.

203

EUDIMOR

Eudimorphodon was discovered in the early 1970s in Cene, near the city of Bergamo in northern Italy, and is considered one of the oldest known pterosaurs. It had a long, bony tail with a flap of skin on the end, which helped it turn quickly while flying. Several skeletons of this species have been found, including many young specimens. Due to the shape of its sternum, this pterosaur may have even been able to flap its wings.

THE TEETH DEBATE

This animal had more than one hundred teeth packed inside a mouth less than 3 inches (8 cm) long, but they weren't all the same. It had long, sharp teeth toward the front, while those at the back were smaller with more **cusps**, and there were also six protruding fangs at the front (four in the upper jaw, and two in the lower one). The top and bottom teeth met each other when the jaws were closed. This amount of **dental occlusion** is the most among the pterosaurs and was perfect for catching fish. Dental wear shows that *Eudimorphodon* also fed on hard-shelled invertebrates and was able to chew food somewhat.

DISTINCTIVE FEATURES: two different types of teeth

...PHODON

Its name means:
TWO FORMS OF TEETH

WHERE IT LIVED:

Europe

ITS WEIGHT:

4.4 lb. (2 kg)

ITS SIZE:

3/3-ft. (1-m) wingspan

WHEN IT LIVED:

220 million years ago

| TRIASSIC | JURASSIC | CRETACEOUS |

SKILLED DIVERS

The large head supported by a stocky neck together with short hand bones have led paleontologists to believe that *Eudimorphodon* had an advanced method of fishing that involved plunge-diving again and again. It grabbed the prey in its mouth like gannets do today. This technique required good eyesight for underwater vision but also very powerful wing muscles to push itself out of the water and fly up into the air.

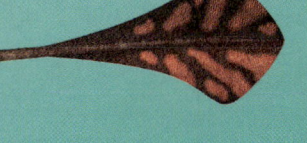

The *Pterodactylus* is bringing freshly caught prey to the nest

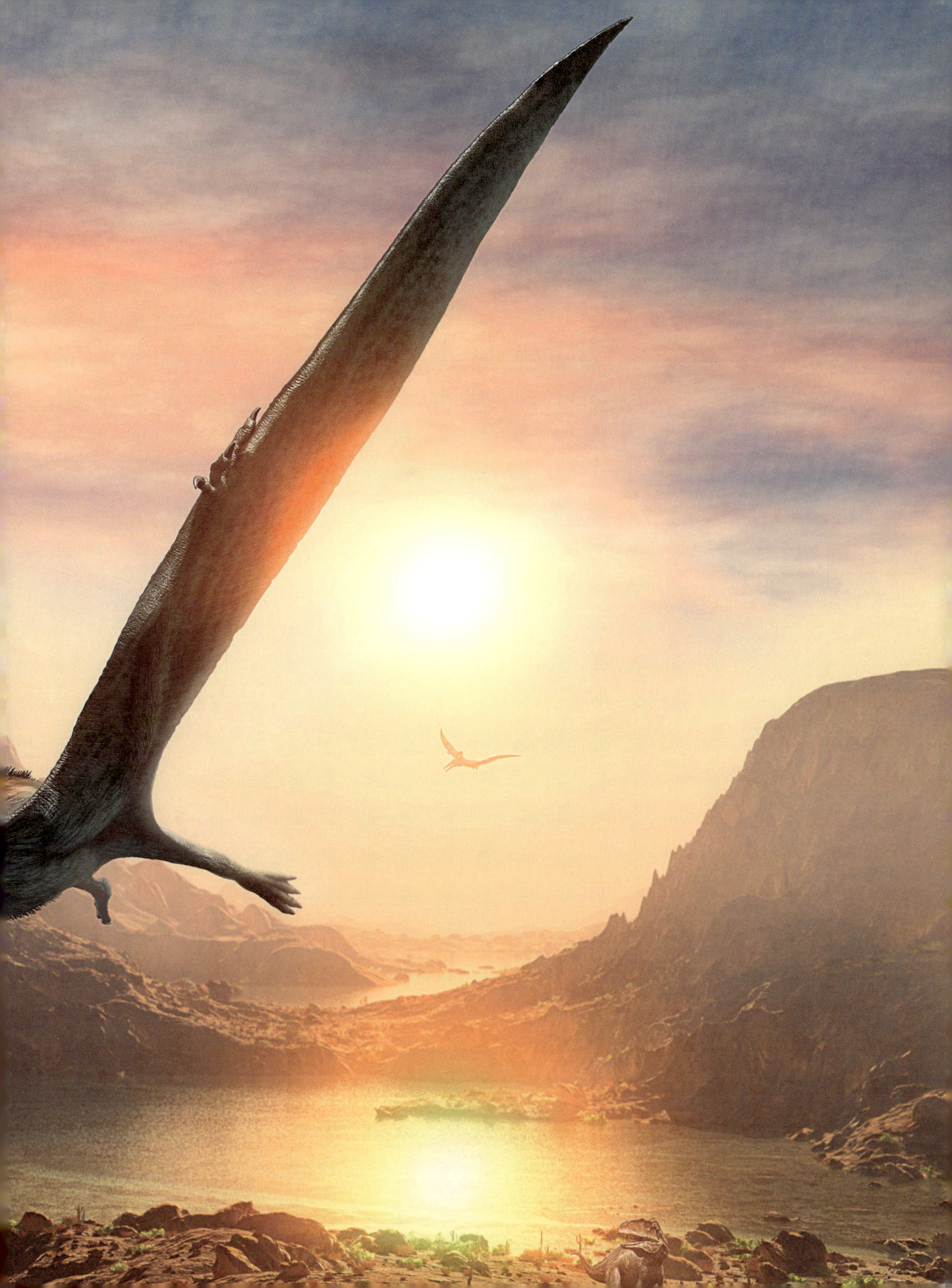

MARINE R

In the Age of Dinosaurs, the oceans were inhabited by reptiles that were perfectly adapted to life in the water. In the Triassic, these animals were widespread in the oceans and rapidly evolved into a variety of shapes and sizes. Some of these early marine reptiles still had legs, so they could come out of the water and live some of the time on the shore, like seals do today. Others, however, were very similar to fish and lived only in the water, although they had to resurface regularly for air. They had lungs instead of gills, so they needed air to survive, as dolphins do. Their bodies were **hydrodynamic**, with fin-like limbs and powerful tails that made them great swimmers.

At the end of the Triassic, about 200 million years ago, a mass extinction wiped out almost all the marine reptiles that ruled the oceans on our planet.

EPTILES

The survivors took a long time to recover, but over the next 135 million years, some of them evolved into the most powerful predators that ever existed.

Their size was just as impressive as that of large carnivorous dinosaurs. Some, like *Pliosaurus* or *Elasmosaurus*, were truly gigantic.

DON'T CALL ME A DINOSAUR
Actually, most marine reptiles belonged to a different branch of the reptile family tree and were more closely related to lizards and snakes than to dinosaurs.

NUMEROUS SWIMMING STYLES
The various species of marine reptiles moved in the water in different ways: some used all four limbs to swim and others just the front ones, using the hind limbs to change direction. Some animals, such as *Ichthyosaurs*, had a powerful tail to push it forward, moving very much like a shark, while their fin-like limbs were used for stability and steering.

Marine reptiles were not dinosaurs, and they were not even part of the reptile group known as the archosaurs

STENOPT

Stenopterygius looked very similar to a tuna fish, although it had a smaller and longer snout. The around one hundred specimens found in England, France, Germany, and other parts of Europe have made it possible to learn a lot about this marine reptile, from its shape and color to its habits. The information obtained from the skeletons suggests it could have been between 10 and 14 feet (3–4 m) long, depending on the species, it had two pectoral fins and two ventral fins, and the end of the vertebral column curved downward.

However, more details about *Stenopterygius* were collected from the best-preserved fossils, such as those found in the Holzmaden fossil deposit in Germany, where even the very delicate parts of the reptile were preserved. In addition to the bones, some of these specimens show the imprint of the animal's body, as if a line were drawn around it. This is how we learned that *Stenopterygius* also had a large fin on its back, which was impossible to see in the skeletons because the fin had no bones, and that its tail was neither straight nor curved downward, but was shaped like a crescent moon. The spine curved downward to support the lower part of the caudal fin, while the upper part was supported by cartilage (the exact opposite of the tail structure in sharks). Even some skin was found in some of the fossils, which provided a lot of information about its color: like many fish and cetaceans today, *Stenopterygius* had a dark back and a light-colored belly.

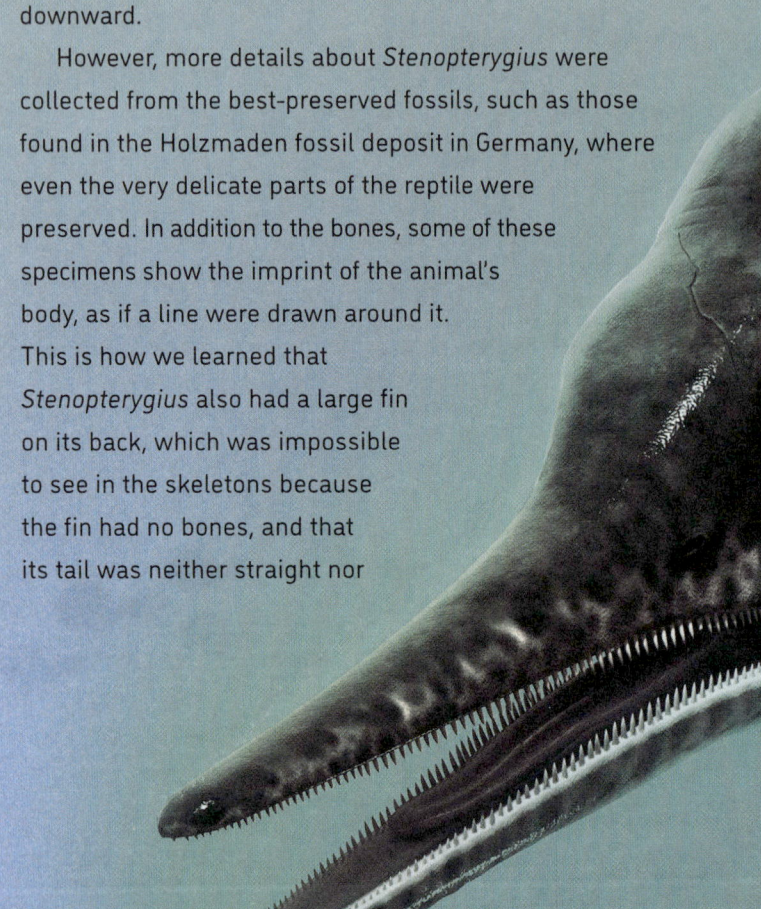

ERYGIUS

Its name means:
NARROW FIN

WHERE IT LIVED:

Europe

ITS WEIGHT:

up to 1,320 lb. (600 kg)

ITS SIZE:

up to 13 ft. (4 m) long

WHEN IT LIVED:

183–175 million years ago

| TRIASSIC | JURASSIC | CRETACEOUS |

DISTINCTIVE FEATURES:
narrow flippers

Its body shape and size were very good for both hunting and defending itself in its environment. It spent most of its time in the open sea and probably attacked its prey—small fish, small reptiles, and **cephalopods** (such as ammonites)—from below so that the dark color of its back would be camouflaged against the darkness of the deep sea. But when it came up to the surface for air, its light belly blended it with the light coming from above, protecting it from predators, which included plesiosaurs.

A FOSSILIZED BIRTH

Some *Stenopterygius* fossils contain the skeletons of **embryos**. These marine reptiles, like many other reptiles, were **ovoviviparous**. This means that although they produced eggs, they did not lay them. Instead they kept them in the abdomen until they hatched, then give birth to perfectly developed calves. One specimen even seems to have been frozen in time at the exact moment of birth: it is an adult female with a calf still halfway inside its body. Like dolphins, *Stenopterygius* gave birth to its calves tail first. In fact, they obtained oxygen from the air, not from the water, so they would have drowned if they came out head first.

213

TYLOSA

Tylosaurus was a marine reptile belonging to the family Mosasauridae, and it was one of its largest members. Its distinctive snout had a knob at the front, making it extremely strong. Since it was found to be damaged in certain fossils, showing marks from repeated impacts and ramming, *Tylosaurus* probably used its reinforced jaw to ram its prey hard enough to stun them.

It may have attacked other marine reptiles as they rose to the surface for air, making them harmless, likely causing them to drown, and therefore easier to devour.

In addition to ramming its prey, we can also assume that *Tylosaurus* used its reinforced **rostrum** to ram other individuals of the same species in order to show who's boss in hunting grounds.

Tylosaurus was a super predator, which means that it was at the top of the marine food chain, and could prey on almost any form of life that crossed its path. Proof of this has been found in the stomach contents of many fossil specimens of these large reptiles, which contained mosasaurs, plesiosaurs, and sharks, but also turtles and ammonites.

Hatchlings did not have the reinforced knob on their jaw, suggesting that they depended more on their teeth than the adults to kill their prey. This was confirmed in 2018, when a one-foot-long skull of a *Tylosaurus* was found without the knob on its snout.

However, they soon began hunting the "adult" way. In fact, the knob was present on skulls that were only slightly larger.

URUS

Its name means: KNOB LIZARD

WHERE IT LIVED:
North America
Europe
Africa

ITS WEIGHT:
7 tons (6,300 kg)

ITS SIZE:
42.6 ft. (13 m) long

DISTINCTIVE FEATURES:
a very long tail and snout with a knob at the front

WHEN IT LIVED:
90–66 million years ago

| TRIASSIC | JURASSIC | CRETACEOUS |

ELASMO

Elasmosaurus was one of the largest marine reptiles, and it certainly had the longest neck, which had over 70 vertebrae and reached a length of 20 feet (6 m). The head may have been so heavy that *Elasmosaurus* could not even lift it out of the water. The neck was not very flexible, so it would have been held mostly straight, and it would only have been able to move slightly from side to side.

Its neck was essential for hunting, since this reptile approached its prey from below, hiding its body in the depths of the sea and then ambushing schools of fish with its long neck. Its U-shaped jaw and sharp, fang-like teeth, which closed like a pincer and locked together, were perfect for spearing and gripping small fish and mollusks. This hunting technique also allowed it to save energy. Although its limbs were like paddles and its body had a hydrodynamic shape, *Elasmosaurus* was not a fast swimmer. Due to its shape, which would have made it very clumsy on land, *Elasmosaurus* probably never came out of the water, not even to lay eggs. Paleontologists think that, like many other marine reptiles, the females of this species carried their eggs inside their abdomen, giving birth to live young.

SAURUS

Its name means:
THIN-PLATED LIZARD

WHERE IT LIVED:

North America

ITS WEIGHT:

3 tons (2,700 kg)

ITS SIZE:

33 ft. (10 m) long

WHEN IT LIVED:

80 million years ago

| TRIASSIC | JURASSIC | CRETACEOUS |

HEADS OR TAILS?

In 1868, the famous paleontologist Edward Cope initially reconstructed *Elasmosaurus* incorrectly by putting the head at the end of the tail. The scientist had mistaken the tail vertebrae for those of the neck, perhaps due to the surprising length of the neck.

This mistake did not go unnoticed by one of his most bitter enemies, the paleontologist Othniel Charles Marsh, who for decades took advantage of every opportunity to point it out. Over the following years the two paleontologists competed with each other for discoveries in the famous "Bone Wars."

DISTINCTIVE FEATURES:
a very long neck

MOSASA

Mosasaurus was an enormous marine reptile with a heavy build. Its limbs were very similar to flippers, while its tail was long, strong, and probably curved downward at the end. The skull tapered toward the tip, and its sharp, cone-shaped teeth, which were continually replaced, were excellent for killing and ripping apart prey. *Mosasaurus*'s size suggests its favorite prey were larger and slower, such as other marine reptiles.

Since the eyes were located on the side of the head, *Mosasaurus* was not able to measure distances between itself and prey, meaning that this ocean giant didn't rely on its speed to chase its victims. The most likely and effective hunting method would probably have been to wait in the upper ocean for other marine reptiles to resurface for air. This would be the easiest moment to attack the prey, as they were in the lightest part of the ocean and unable to dive without first taking a breath of air. *Mosasaurus* could then ambush them by propelling itself with a quick but short flick of the tail. Even if the attack didn't kill the prey, it would at least wound it, and *Mosasaurus* would then have been able to follow it until it got tired.

URUS

Its name means:
LIZARD OF THE MEUSE RIVER

WHERE IT LIVED:
North America
Europe

ITS WEIGHT:
15 tons (13,600 kg)

ITS SIZE:
up to 50 ft. (15 m) long

WHEN IT LIVED:
82.7–66 million years ago

| TRIASSIC | JURASSIC | CRETACEOUS |

Close-up of a *Mosasaurus* tooth

COMBAT BETWEEN MOSASAURS

Many *Mosasaurus* skull fossils show signs of serious injuries, at times fatal and probably caused by an individual of the same species. A *Mosasaurus* skeleton with a tooth from another *Mosasaurus* stuck in the jaw below the eye shows clear evidence of this. There are signs of healing around the wound, showing that the victim survived the attack. Another fossil shows wounds on various bones, especially in the areas around the back of the skull and neck. None of these show any signs of healing, which means the attacker killed the *Mosasaurus* with a fatal blow to the head.

DISTINCTIVE FEATURES: a very long tail

A fight between two *Mosasaurus*

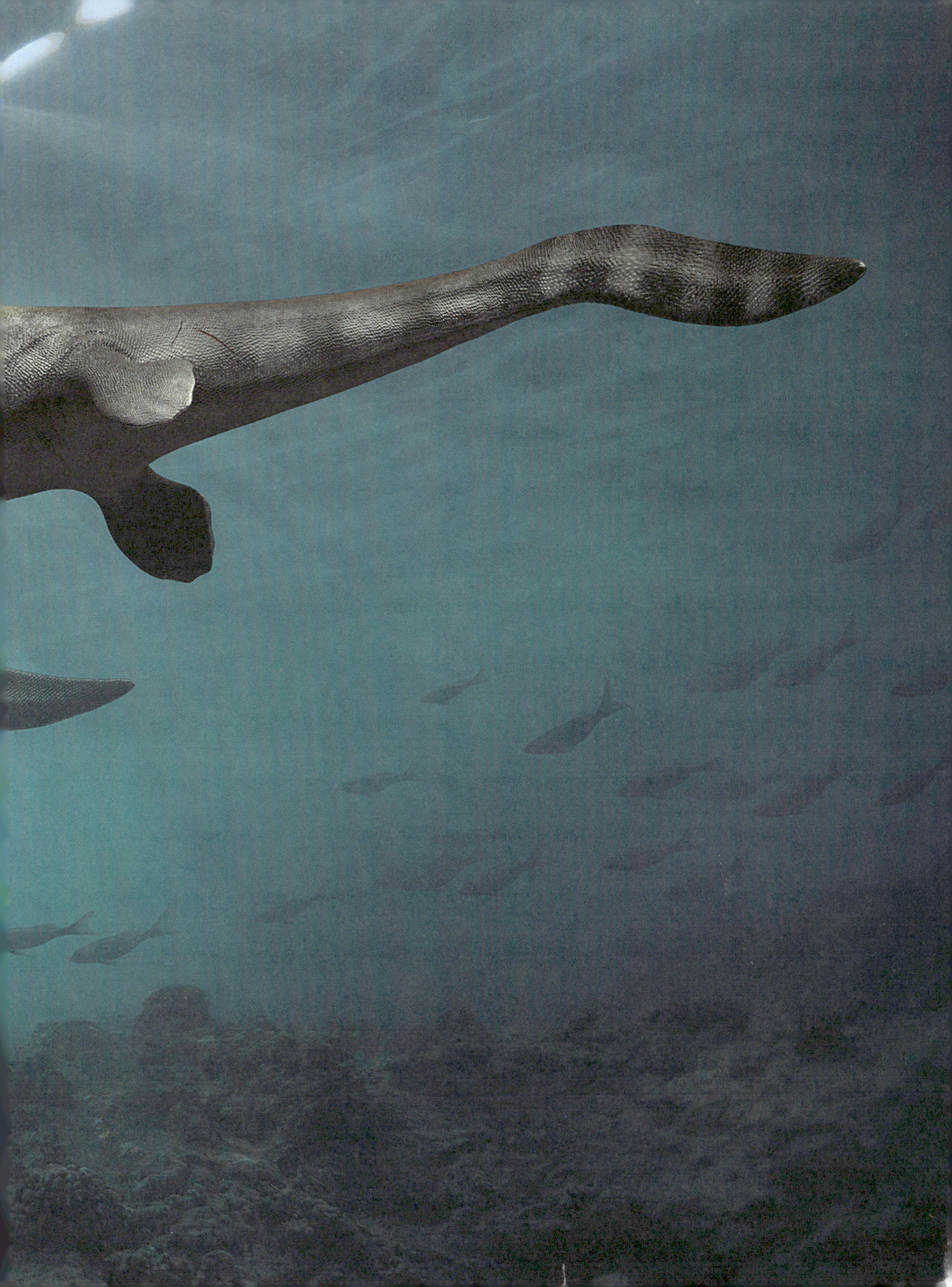

ICHTHYO

Ichthyosaurus is best known for its close resemblance to a fish or dolphin. This shape is the best for moving in the water, but it also prevented *Ichthyosaurus* from getting out of the ocean and onto land. It lived only an aquatic life.

Ichthyosaurs were hunters, and their diet was mainly fish. Fish and squid have been found in their fossilized excrements, called coprolites, confirming their eating habits.

The sense that *Ichthyosaurus* relied on most for hunting was sight, although the solid bone structure of the eardrums suggests that it may have "heard" prey from a distance, thanks to vibrations in the water.

Some specimens have revealed that ichthyosaurs did not lay eggs but gave birth to live calves, like dolphins, which came out of the mother's body tail first so they would not drown during birth.

DISTINCTIVE FEATURES: a tapered snout and a dorsal fin

SAURUS

Its name means:
FISH LIZARD

WHERE IT LIVED:

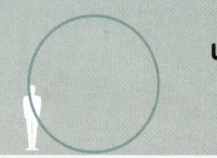

Europe

ITS WEIGHT:

up to 1 ton (900 kg)

ITS SIZE:

10.8 ft. (3.3 m) long

WHEN IT LIVED:

200–190 million years ago

| TRIASSIC | JURASSIC | CRETACEOUS |

THE FOSSIL HUNTER

The first *Ichthyosaurus* skeleton was found by Mary Anning, although the skull was found first by her older brother, who had just turned 15 years old, in the cliffs in Lyme Regis, England, in 1811. The skull was first thought to have belonged to a crocodile, but when Mary unearthed the rest of the skeleton a few months later, it was reclassified, and the naturalist Charles Konig gave it the name *Ichthyosaurus*. Mary was only 12 years old at the time, but over the following years she found more *Ichthyosaurus* fossils, many other species of marine reptiles, and the first flying reptile in England.

PLIOSAU

The first fossil of *Pliosaurus* was described in 1841 by Richard Owen, the paleontologist who coined the term *dinosaur*. This reptile was one of the scariest predators of its time.

Unlike its long-necked relatives, *Pliosaurus* had a very large head good for hunting a wide range of small and large prey, such as other marine reptiles. Its preference for large animals is shown by its teeth, which were up to 12 inches (30 cm) long, and massive jaws, making its bite extremely powerful and effective against large prey such as plesiosaurs, ichthyosaurs, smaller pliosaurs, and probably giant fish.

It used its sharp, sturdy front teeth to pierce and kill its victims, while its back teeth were used to push food into its throat.

DISTINCTIVE FEATURES:
a very large head compared to the body

RUS

Its name means:
MORE LIZARD

WHERE IT LIVED:

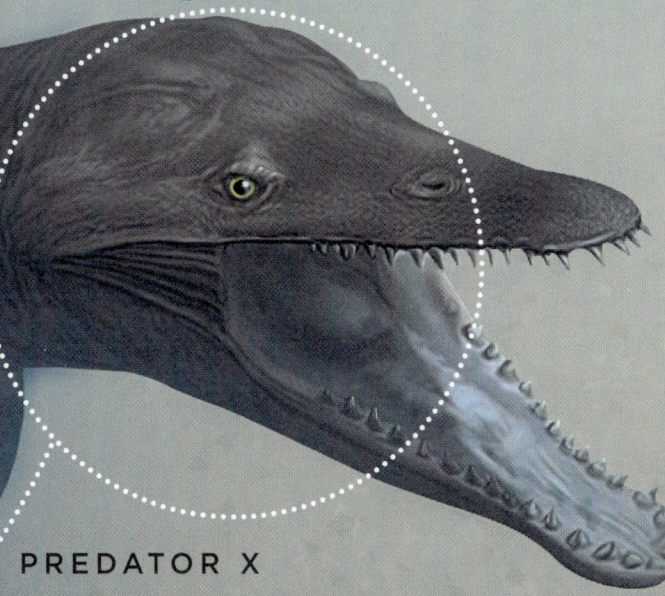

Europe
South America

ITS WEIGHT:

6–10 tons (5,000–9,000 kg)

ITS SIZE:

33–42.6 ft. (10–13 m) long

WHEN IT LIVED:

156–147 million years ago

| TRIASSIC | JURASSIC | CRETACEOUS |

Unlike most dinosaurs, *Pliosauruses* had curved teeth

PREDATOR X

In 2006, fossil pieces of a marine reptile were unearthed on an island in the Arctic archipelago, or collection of islands, of Svalbard. There were an incredible 20,000 pieces! The pieces were put together slowly, just like a jigsaw puzzle, and the result was an enormous *Pliosaurus*, 50 feet (15 m) long, which was nicknamed "Predator X." Today Predator X has a scientific name, *Pliosaurus funkei*, and it is now estimated to have been only between 33 and 42 feet (10–12.8 m) long. Despite having been "shortened," Predator X is still the largest *Pliosaurus* known to date.

225

PLESIOS

The debate about the *Plesiosaurus* tail is still on! Some specimens show evidence of a small fin, but scholars do not agree on its shape

DISTINCTIVE FEATURES: a long neck and a stubby tail

"A snake threaded through the shell of a turtle." This is how *Plesiosaurus* was described in the early 19th century when paleontologist Mary Anning discovered the first specimens in the cliffs in Lyme Regis, England. Although plesiosaurs have nothing that resembles a turtle shell, this is actually a pretty good description. It was a reptile with a long neck and a small head, a broad body, and a short, stubby tail. Its four legs, which were used as paddles, were very similar to those of turtles. On each of its limbs were five digits, and each of those had a very high number of **phalanges**, or individual finger or toe bones.

Because it used all four limbs to swim, *Plesiosaurus* was not very fast, although it was certainly very agile. And with a mouth packed with pointed teeth, it was probably a dangerous predator, although it seemed to mainly hunt fish and cephalopods, such as ammonites. *Plesiosaurus* were ovoviviparous, but unlike other marine reptiles, they probably only gave birth to single young.

AURUS

Its name means:
ALMOST A LIZARD

WHERE IT LIVED:

Europe

ITS WEIGHT:

992 lb. (450 kg)

ITS SIZE:

11-16.5 ft. (3.5-5m) long

WHEN IT LIVED:

199.6–175.6 million years ago

| TRIASSIC | JURASSIC | CRETACEOUS |

A LONG NECK

Plesiosaurus is very often shown with its neck raised out of the water, supple and flexible like a swan's, but studies on the vertebrae have revealed that it was actually quite stiff. And even if it could lift the weight of its neck, it would still not have been able to maintain an ideal swimming position, as the entire animal would have leaned forward. Therefore, the neck was probably held straight in front of the body, only bending sideways.

227

LIOPLEU

Liopleurodon's most notable characteristics were its very large skull, which was about one-fifth of the total body length, and short tail. The size of the skull and the teeth set deeply in the jaws suggest that this marine reptile had a very powerful bite. Its paddle-like limbs meant that it couldn't move very fast, but it could swim quickly in short bursts, making it an excellent hunter. Its nostrils also made it the perfect predator. Studies on the skull have shown that their position allowed Liopleurodon to find prey outside its field of vision, perhaps even smelling the blood of animals injured by other predators.

DISTINCTIVE FEATURES: a very large head compared to the body

RODON

Its name means:
SMOOTH-SIDED TEETH

WHERE IT LIVED:

Europe

ITS WEIGHT:

3 tons (2,700 kg)

ITS SIZE:

19.7–23 ft. (6–7 m) long

WHEN IT LIVED:

166–155 million years ago

TRIASSIC	JURASSIC	CRETACEOUS

MADELEINE THE ROBOT

An underwater robot named Madeleine has helped scientists understand the swimming patterns of many of today's animals, such as sea turtles and penguins, but also of extinct specimens like *Liopleurodon* and other plesiosaurs. They found that the robot's speed did not increase when it used four flippers instead of two, perhaps because the front flippers created turbulence that interfered with the back flippers' ability to push it forward. However, Madeleine was able to make quicker starts and stops with all four limbs.

Paleontologists then hypothesized that plesiosaurs, unlike today's animals, used all four flippers to swim in order to take advantage of the rapid increase in speed to ambush prey.

EXTINC

Extinction is the final disappearance of a living species. Although we don't realize it, dozens of species go extinct every day. But sometimes there are events that lead to the sudden disappearance of thousands of species at the same time. Due to the number of species they affect, these are called mass extinctions.

TION

At least five mass extinctions have occurred in the history of life on Earth, and two of these killed off the dinosaurs. The first marked the start of the Mesozoic era, 252 million years ago, and the second marked its end 66 million years ago.

The first was the most catastrophic, or a disaster, but the second is the most famous because it was "the extinction of the dinosaurs." This event caused the disappearance of three out of four life forms and is more well known because the dinosaurs were among them.

There has been a long-standing debate on what caused it, but there have always been only two possibilities: the impact of a gigantic meteorite or extremely violent volcanic eruptions. Both of these hypotheses are supported by evidence. All over the world, there is an element called iridium in the rocks that formed 66 million years ago, which is very rare in Earth's crust but extremely common in meteorites. And in India, there are lava flows covering an area of nearly 200,000 square miles (500,000 sq km), which have been dated to around the end of the Cretaceous.

More recent studies, together with the discovery of a giant crater near the town of Chicxulub, Mexico, in the 1990s, which was 112 miles (180 km) across, have tipped the scales toward a meteorite being the main cause of this mass extinction.

Therefore, 66 million years ago, a 9-mile-wide (15 km) object from space impacted our planet, triggering a series of events that upset its balance: fires, earthquakes, and tsunamis are just a few examples, along with the dust from where the crater hit Earth, which polluted the atmosphere and completely blocked the sun.

The climate changed dramatically and the plants disappeared, leading to the death of the herbivores, which in turn led to the carnivores starving. Also, the oceans became acidic and unlivable.

This catastrophe led to the disappearance of all flying reptiles, almost all marine reptiles, and all non-avian dinosaurs. Although severely affected, some species of non-dinosaur land reptiles, birds (avian dinosaurs), crocodiles, turtles, and mammals were spared.

The mammals did what the reptiles had done before them: they adapted and conquered all the environments that had become available.

THEME PARKS

There is no better place to learn more about dinosaurs, observe their remains, and see life-size reconstructions than natural history museums, which preserve and exhibit collections of life-size fossils and skeletons. Theme parks, on the other hand, are either built on fossil sites, where the remains of dinosaurs can be seen still embedded in the rocks, or are recreational parks where you can see realistic models of dinosaurs as well as enjoy other leisure activities. Below and on the next page you will find a list of the most important museums and theme parks in the world, along with their websites.

DINOSAURIER PARK (MÜNCHEHAGEN, GERMANY)
www.dinopark.de

ROARR! DINOSAUR ADVENTURE (NORFOLK, UNITED KINGDOM)
www.roarrdinosauradventure.co.uk

DINOSAUR NATIONAL MONUMENT (JENSEN, UTAH, USA)
www.nps.gov/dino/index.htm

PRÉHISTO-DINO PARC (LACAVE EN QUERCY, FRANCE)
prehistodino.com

GONDWANA – DAS PRAEHISTORIUM (SCHIFFWEILER, GERMANY)
www.gondwana-das-praehistorium.de

DINOSAUR LAND (RÜGEN, GERMANY)
www.dinosaurierland-ruegen.de

PARCO DELLA PREHISTORIA (RIVOLTA D'ADDA, ITALY)
www.parcodellapreistoria.it

DINO PARQUE (LOURINHA, PORTUGAL)
www.dinoparque.pt

ECO PARK (BAGUIO, PHILIPPINES)
baguiocityguide.com/visiting-the-bamboo-eco-park-in-baguio-kyoto-in-baguio/

AMERICAN MUSEUM OF NATURAL HISTORY (NEW YORK, NEW YORK, USA)
www.amnh.org

DINOSAUR VALLEY STATE PARK (GLEN ROSE, TEXAS, USA)
tpwd.texas.gov/state-parks/dinosaur-valley

DINOPARK FUNTANA (ISTRIA, CROATIA)
dinopark.hr

AND MUSEUMS AROUND THE WORLD

MUSEO CIVICO DI STORIA NATURALE (MILAN, ITALY)

museodistorianaturalemilano.it

MUSEO DEL JURÁSICO DE ASTURIAS (COLUNGA, SPAIN)

www.museojurasicoasturias.com

MUSEUM FÜR NATURKUNDE (BERLIN, GERMANY)

www.museumfuernaturkunde.berlin

FIELD MUSEUM (CHICAGO, ILLINOIS, USA)

www.fieldmuseum.org

NATURAL HISTORY MUSEUM (LONDON, UNITED KINGDOM)

www.nhm.ac.uk

ROYAL BELGIAN INSTITUTE OF NATURAL SCIENCES (BRUSSELS, BELGIUM)

www.naturalsciences.be

ROYAL TYRRELL MUSEUM OF PALENTOLOGY (DRUMHELLER, ALBERTA, CANADA)

tyrrellmuseum.com

THE CHILDREN'S MUSEUM (INDIANAPOLIS, INDIANA, USA)

www.childrensmuseum.org

NATIONAL DINOSAUR MUSEUM (CANBERRA, AUSTRALIA)

nationaldinosaurmuseum.com.au

WYOMING DINOSAUR CENTER (THERMOPOLIS, WYOMING, USA)

wyomingdinosaurcenter.org

MUSEO PALEOLAB DI PIETRAROJA (PIETRAROJA, ITALY)

www.entegeopaleontologico.it

IZIKO MUSEUMS (CAPE TOWN, SOUTH AFRICA)

www.iziko.org.za

FERNBANK MUSEUM OF NATURAL HISTORY (ATLANTA, GEORGIA, USA)

www.fernbankmuseum.org

SMITHSONIAN MUSEUM OF NATURAL HISTORY (WASHINGTON, DC, USA)

naturalhistory.si.edu

FUKUI PREFECTURAL DINOSAUR MUSEUM (KATSUYAMA, JAPAN)

www.dinosaur.pref.fukui.jp/en

NATIONAL MUSEUM OF NATURAL HISTORY (PARIS, FRANCE)

www.mnhn.fr/en

GLOSSARY

AERODYNAMIC FORCE - The force on a solid object as it moves through a fluid (liquid or gas) such as air.

AMBUSH - A hunting technique that involves catching prey by surprise.

ARBOREAL - Describes an animal that lives in trees.

ARTHROPODS - Invertebrate animals such as insects, spiders, scorpions, and crustaceans, whose limbs are divided into jointed segments.

BEAK - A long or pointed horny structure that covers the front part of the jaws.

BILIVERDIN - A green pigment produced by the body.

BINOCULAR VISION - When an image is seen by both eyes at the same time. It is typical in animals with forward-facing eyes and makes it possible to accurately calculate distances.

BONY FRILL - A bony structure on the back of an animal's skull that covers at least part of its neck.

CANNIBALISM - The practice of eating members of one's own species.

CARCASS - The remains of an animal from which most of the flesh has already been torn off.

CASSOWARY - A large, flightless bird with black feathers and a blue, featherless head with a large crest.

CEPHALOPODS - Marine mollusks like today's octopus, cuttlefish, and squid, or ammonites (now extinct).

CLAW - The last bone of a finger; it is curved, pointed, and covered with a strong nail that is also curved and pointed.

COLLAGEN - An organic substance present in the soft tissue of an organism that connects, supports, and feeds the various organs in the body.

COPROLITE - Fossilized feces.

CREST - A bony, fleshy, or feathery protuberance usually found on the heads of certain birds, reptiles, and fish.

CT SCAN - A technique similar to an X-ray, mainly used to diagnose medical conditions. It gets very detailed images of the inside of the body, from which it is possible to reconstruct a three-dimensional model.

CUSP - A point on the crown of a tooth.

DECOMPOSITION - A process that attacks the body of any living organism after death, starting with the flesh, eventually destroying it completely.

DENTAL OCCLUSION - The alignment of the upper and lower teeth when the mouth is closed.

DINOSAURS - A group of land reptiles with columnar limbs, that is, straight and upright under the body. The Mesozoic dinosaurs, which became extinct 66 million years ago, are called non-avian dinosaurs, to differentiate them from avian dinosaurs, which still exist today and are commonly called birds.

DISPLAY - A set of characteristics or behaviors used by animals to communicate with members of the same species or with different species.

EMBRYO - The early stage of development of an organism, immediately after an egg is fertilized.

ERA - One of the divisions of the geologic time scale. The beginning and end of an era are identified by events, such as a mass extinction, and eras are divided into periods.

FIN - A structure that helps animals to move or have greater stability in water.

FLAPPING FLIGHT - A flight mode that involves the continuous flapping of the wings.

FOSSIL - The remains or trace of an organism from the past, usually transformed into rock.

FOSSILIZATION - The process that preserves the remains or traces of organisms from the past.

FRUGIVORE - An herbivorous animal that mainly eats fruit.

GASTROLITHS - Stones that some animals digest to grind food in the stomach.

GLIDING FLIGHT - A flight mode that involves keeping the wings open in one position.

HERD - A group of animals that live and work together to hunt or raise their young.

HORNS - Hard, often pointed structures on an animal's head, made of bone or other substances such as keratin.

HYDRODYNAMIC - Describes an object or animal that is able to move easily in water.

KERATIN - The organic substance that hair and nails are made of.

LACUSTRINE - Related to or associated with lakes.

LUNG CAPACITY - The maximum amount of air the lungs can hold.

MAMMALS - Vertebrate animals that breastfeed their young.

MANDIBLE - A U-shaped bone in the skull that holds the lower dental arch. It is also called the lower jaw.

MATING RITUALS - Set of behaviors that an animal uses to get a mate for reproducing.

MAXILLA - The part of the skull that holds the upper dental arch.

NESTING AREA - An area chosen by animals to lay their eggs and raise their young.

NEURAL SPINE - A bony bulge on the vertebrae of some animals that usually supports a sail or a hump.

ORNITHISCHIANS - Bipedal or quadrupedal herbivorous dinosaurs with pelvis bones similar to those of today's birds. This group includes stegosaurs, ankylosaurs, and ceratopsids.

OSTEODERMS - Rigid structures made of bony plates, keratin, or thick, leathery skin, found on the skin of some animals, such as crocodiles, that are usually for protection.

OVOVIVIPAROUS - Describes an animal that produces eggs but does not lay them, leaving them to hatch inside its body and then giving birth to live young.

PALEONTOLOGY - The scientific study of prehistoric life based on fossils.

PANGAEA - The supercontinent that incorporated almost all the landmasses on Earth and existed between the Late Paleozoic and the Jurassic.

PATAGIUM - A membrane of skin that stretches between the body and limbs, like those of bats or pterosaurs, allowing the animal to move through the air.

PERIOD - A unit of geologic time used to divide an era into smaller time intervals.

PHALANGES - The group of bones that make up the fingers of each hand and work with each other.

PISCIVORE - A carnivorous animal that mainly eats fish.

PRINT - A mark left in the ground by any part of an animal's body or a plant and that shows its characteristics.

PROTOPORPHYRIN - A substance produced by the body that gives eggs a brown color.

PTEROSAURS - Mesozoic reptiles that could fly because of wings formed by an extremely long finger and a membrane of skin.

PYCNOFIBERS - Hair-like filaments similar to primitive feathers that covered certain parts of pterosaurs' bodies.

PYGOSTYLE - The end of a bird's spinal column where the final four or five vertebrae are fused together, which supports the long tail feathers.

QUADRUPEDS - Animals that walk on all fours.

QUILL FEATHERS - Rigid structures, composed mainly of keratin, found on the wings and tails of birds. They can be very colorful and they create a large surface that allows flight.

ROSTRUM - A bulging structure found at the front of the mouth in some animals.

SAIL - A tall, wide structure on the back of some animals, consisting of a membrane of skin that is usually supported by neural spines.

SCALES - Thick, horny structures that cover the bodies of reptiles and some small areas of birds and are very rarely found on mammals.

SCAVENGER - An animal that feeds on the remains of animals hunted and killed by another animal.

SCLEROTIC RINGS - Bony structures around the eye socket that support the eyeball. They are found in birds, aquatic animals, and dinosaurs, but not in mammals.

SEDIMENT - Solid materials such as mud, sand, or gravel.

SKULL - A bone structure that forms the head of an animal.

STERNUM - A bone in the chest to which the ribs are attached. It can be very well developed in flying animals, as the pectoral muscles used to flap the wings are also attached to it.

THEROPOD - This term means "beast-footed" and is one of a group of mostly carnivorous dinosaurs.

TRACE FOSSIL - A type of fossil that shows evidence of the activity of a living being without showing any part of its body. Traces can be footprints, coprolites, eggs, bitemarks, and more.

WINGS - Limbs that make it possible to stay in the air.

ALPHABETICAL ORDER OF DINOSAURS

Acrocanthosaurus	78	Eudimorphodon	204	Protoceratops	120
Alamosaurus	98	Gallimimus	82	Pteranodon	188
Allosaurus	56	Giganotosaurus	38	Pterodactylus	194
Altirhinus	174	Guanlong	26	Puertasaurus	102
Amargasaurus	160	Ichthyosaurus	222	Quetzalcoatlus	184
Ankylosaurus	146	Ichthyovenator	64	Rhamphorhynchus	196
Apatosaurus	134	Iguanodon	176	Spinosaurus	66
Archaeopteryx	90	Lambeosaurus	166	Stegosaurus	170
Argentinosaurus	150	Liopleurodon	228	Stenopterygius	210
Austroraptor	74	Maiasaura	142	Stygimoloch	140
Baryonyx	70	Microraptor	34	Tapejara	200
Carnotaurus	30	Mosasaurus	218	Therizinosaurus	168
Ceratosaurus	62	Ouranosaurus	158	Torosaurus	108
Citipati	36	Oviraptor	48	Triceratops	104
Deinonychus	24	Pachycephalosaurus	136	Troodon	52
Diabloceratops	116	Pachyrhinosaurus	126	Tupandactylus	202
Dilophosaurus	28	Parasaurolophus	154	Tylosaurus	214
Diplodocus	130	Plateosaurus	164	Tyrannosaurus	84
Einiosaurus	112	Plesiosaurus	226	Velociraptor	42
Elasmosaurus	216	Pliosaurus	224		

IMAGE CREDITS

pp. 2–3 - Daniel Eskridge/Shutterstock; **pp. 4–5** - Herschel Hoffmeyer/Shutterstock; **pp. 8–9** - Dani el Eskridge/Shutterstock; **p. 10 top** - Catmando/Shutterstock; **pp. 10–11** - bortonia/Getty Images; **pp. 14–15** - JoeLena/Getty Images; **pp. 16–17** - Daniel Eskridge/Shutterstock; **pp. 18–19** - Daniel Eskridge/Shutterstock; **pp. 20–21** - Daniel Eskridge/Shutterstock; **p. 22** - DM7/Shutterstock; **p. 23** - Jon Hicks/Getty Images; **pp. 24–25** - Valentyna Chukhlyebova/Alamy Stock Photo; **p. 25** - Dorling Kindersley ltd/Alamy Stock Photo; **p. 26** - Zhongda Zhang/Getty Images; **pp. 28–29** - Daniel Eskridge/Shutterstock; **pp. 30–31** - DM7/Shutterstock; **pp. 32–33** - Daniel Eskridge/Shutterstock; **p. 34** - Stocktrek Images, Inc./Alamy Stock Photo; **p. 35** - Steve Vidler/Alamy Stock Photo; **p. 36** - Daniel Eskridge/Shutterstock; **pp. 38–39** - Leonello Calvetti/Alamy Stock Photo; **p. 38 bottom** - Leonello Calvetti/Alamy Stock Photo; **pp. 40–41** - Daniel Eskridge/Shutterstock; **pp. 42–43** - Herschel Hoffmeyer/Shutterstock; **p. 43 bottom** - Leonello Calvetti/Alamy Stock Photo; **p. 44 top** - Filippo Vanzo/Shutterstock; **p. 44 bottom** - Dinoton/Shutterstock; **p. 45 top** - Walter Geiersperger/Getty Images; **p. 45 bottom** - Natalia van D/Shutterstock; **pp. 46–47** - Daniel Eskridge/Getty Images; **pp. 48–49** - Julius Csotonyi/Novapix/Bridgeman Images; **p. 50 left** - Alan Curtis/Alamy Stock Photo; **pp. 50–51** - Julius Csotonyi/Novapix/Bridgeman Images; **p. 52** - Catmando/Shutterstock; **p. 53 left** - Catmando/Shutterstock; **p. 53 right** - The Natural History Museum/Alamy Stock Photo; **pp. 54–55** - Raul Lunia/Novapix/Bridgeman Images; **pp. 56–57** - Leonello Calvetti/Alamy Stock Photo; **p. 57 bottom** - Leonello Calvetti/Alamy Stock Photo; **p. 58** - The Natural History Museum/Alamy Stock Photo; **p. 59 top** - dpa picture alliance/Alamy Stock Photo; **p. 59 bottom** - Love Lego/Shutterstock; **pp. 60–61** - MasPix/Alamy Stock Photo; **pp. 62–63** - Roman Garcia Mora; **pp. 64–65** - Stocktrek Images, Inc./Alamy Stock Photo; **pp. 66–67** - Herschel Hoffmeyer/Shutterstock; **p. 68** - Lakeview Image/Shutterstock; **p. 69** - Mohamad Haghani/Alamy Stock Photo; **pp. 70–71** - Stocktrek Images,

/Alamy Stock Photo; **p. 72 top** - The Natural History Museum/Alamy Stock Photo; **pp. 72-73 top** - The Natural History Museum/Alamy Stock Photo; **pp. 72-73 bottom** - Daniel Eskridge/Shutterstock; **p. 74** - Catmando/Shutterstock; **pp. 76-77** - Elenarts/Shutterstock; **p. 78** - Warpaint/Shutterstock; **p. 80** - Catmando/Shutterstock; **p. 81** - Michael Rosskothen/Shutterstock; **p. 82 top** - Dorling Kindersley ltd/Alamy Stock Photo; **pp. 82-83** - Stocktrek Images, Inc./Alamy Stock Photo; **p. 83 bottom** - Dorling Kindersley ltd/Alamy Stock Photo; **pp. 84-85** - Matis75/Shutterstock; **p. 85** - Puwadol Jaturawutthichai/Shutterstock; **pp. 86-87** - Antic Andrej /EyeEm/Getty Images; **p. 87 top** - Walter Geiersperger/Getty Images; **pp. 88-89** - wwing/Getty Images; **p. 90** - Daniel Eskridge/Shutterstock; **p. 91** - Martin Shields/Alamy Stock Photo; **pp. 92, 93** - Leonello Calvetti/Alamy Stock Photo; **p. 94** - Daniel Eskridge/Shutterstock; **p. 95** - Daniel Eskridge/Shutterstock; **p. 96** - Diego Mattarelli; **pp. 96-97** center - DM7/Shutterstock; **p. 97 left top** - The Natural History Museum/Alamy Stock Photo; **p. 97 left bottom** - Diego Mattarelli; **p. 97 right top** - Diego Mattarelli; **p. 97 right bottom** - The Natural History Museum/Alamy Stock Photo; **pp. 98-99** - Herschel Hoffmeyer/Shutterstock; **pp. 100-101** - Herschel Hoffmeyer/Shutterstock; **pp. 102-103** - Herschel Hoffmeyer/Shutterstock; **pp. 104-105** - Dotted Yeti/Shutterstock; **pp. 106-107** - Matis75/Shutterstock; **p. 107 top** - Dan Kitwood/Getty Images; **p. 107 bottom** - Ton Bangkeaw/Shutterstock; **p. 108** - Daniel Eskridge/Shutterstock; **pp. 110-111** - Raul Lunia/Novapix/Bridgeman Images; **pp. 112-113** - ExpressionImage/Shutterstock; **pp. 114-115** - Stocktrek Images, Inc./Alamy Stock Photo; **pp. 116-117** - DM7/Alamy Stock Photo; **p. 118 left** - Stocktrek Images, Inc./Alamy Stock Photo; **pp. 118-119** - Novapix/Bridgeman Images; **p. 120** - Yuriy Priymak/Stocktrek Images/Getty Images; **p. 122** - The Natural History Museum/Alamy Stock Photo; **p. 123** - Warpaint/Shutterstock; **pp. 124-125** - MasPix/Alamy Stock Photo; **pp. 126-127** - Corey Ford/Alamy Stock Photo; **pp. 128-129** - MasPix/Alamy Stock Photo; **p. 130** - Herschel Hoffmeyer/Shutterstock; **pp. 132-133 top** - Leonello Calvetti/Alamy Stock Photo; **pp. 132-133 bottom** - Leonello Calvetti/Alamy Stock Photo; **p. 133** - INTERFOTO/Alamy Stock Photo; **pp. 134-135** - Daniel Eskridge/Shutterstock; **p. 135 bottom** - Loop Images/Getty Images; **pp. 136-137** - Daniel Eskridge/Shutterstock; **p. 137** - Science Photo Library/Alamy Stock Photo; **pp. 138-139** - Daniel Eskridge/Shutterstock; **pp. 140-141** - Stocktrek Images, Inc./Alamy Stock Photo; **pp. 142-143** - Leonello Calvetti/Alamy Stock Photo; **pp. 144-145** - De Agostini Picture Library/Getty Images; **p. 145 top** - Roberto Nistri/Alamy Stock Photo; **p. 146 top** - Warpaint/Shutterstock; **p. 146 bottom** - Leonello Calvetti/Alamy Stock Photo; **pp. 148-149** - Daniel Eskridge/Shutterstock; **pp. 150-151** - Elenarts/Shutterstock; **pp. 152-153** - Michael Rosskothen/Shutterstock; **p. 154** - Noiel/Shutterstock; **p. 155** - imageBROKER/Alamy Stock Photo; **pp. 156-157** - MasPix/Alamy Stock Photo; **pp. 158-159** - Herschel Hoffmeyer/Shutterstock; **pp. 160-161** - Roman Garcia Mora; **pp. 162-163** - Danita Delimont/Alamy Stock Photo; **p. 164** - Michael Rosskothen/Shutterstock; **p. 165** - Breckeni/Getty Images; **p. 166** - Warpaint/Shutterstock; **p. 167** - Reimar/Shutterstock; **pp. 168-169** - Herschel Hoffmeyer/Shutterstock; **p. 169** - Walter Geiersperger/Getty Images; **pp. 170-171** - Roman Garcia Mora; **pp. 172-173** - Love Lego/Shutterstock; **pp. 174-175** - Daniel Eskridge/Shutterstock; **pp. 176-177** - Leonello Calvetti/Alamy Stock Photo; **p. 177 bottom** - The Natural History Museum/Alamy Stock Photo; **p. 178** - Danny Ye/Shutterstock; **pp. 178-179** - The Natural History Museum/Alamy Stock Photo; **p. 179** - The Natural History Museum/Alamy Stock Photo; **pp. 180-181** - Daniel Eskridge/Alamy Stock Photo; **pp. 182-183** - Science Photo Library/Alamy Stock Photo; **pp. 184-185** - Michael Rosskothen/Shutterstock; **p. 186 left** - Corbin17/Alamy Stock Photo; **pp. 186-187** - Michael Rosskothen/Shutterstock; **pp. 188-189** - Stocktrek Images, Inc./Alamy Stock Photo; **p. 189 bottom** - The Washington Post/Getty Images; **pp. 190-191** - ValentynaChukhlyebova/Shutterstock; **p. 191 right top** - Herschel Hoffmeyer/Shutterstock; **pp. 192-193** - Stocktrek Images, Inc./Alamy Stock Photo; **pp. 194-195** - Corey Ford/Alamy Stock Photo; **pp. 196-197** - Michael Rosskothen/Shutterstock; **p. 198 left** - ER Degginger/Alamy Stock Photo; **pp. 198-199 top** - Corey Ford/Alamy Stock Photo; **pp. 198-199 bottom** - Warpaint/Shutterstock; **p. 200** - Stocktrek Images, Inc./Alamy Stock Photo; **pp. 202, 203** - Stocktrek Images, Inc./Alamy Stock Photo; **pp. 204, 205** - Leonello Calvetti/Alamy Stock Photo; **pp. 206-207** - Warpaint/Shutterstock; **pp. 208-209** - Mohamad Haghani/Alamy Stock Photo; **pp. 210-211** - Warpaint/Shutterstock; **pp. 212-213** - MasPix/Alamy Stock Photo; **p. 213 top** - The Natural History Museum/Alamy Stock Photo; **pp. 214-215** - Stocktrek Images, Inc./Alamy Stock Photo; **p. 216** - Andreas Meyer/Shutterstock; **p. 217** - Stocktrek Images, Inc./Alamy Stock Photo; **p. 218** - Stocktrek Images, Inc./Alamy Stock Photo; **p. 219 top** - Ryan M. Bolton/Shutterstock; **p. 219 bottom** - Phil Degginger/Alamy Stock Photo; **pp. 220-221** - Mohamad Haghani/Alamy Stock Photo; **pp. 222-223** - MasPix/Alamy Stock Photo; **pp. 224-225** - Nobumichi Tamura/Stocktrek Images/Getty Images; **p. 225 right bottom** - The Natural History Museum/Alamy Stock Photo; **p. 226** - Roman Garcia Mora; **p. 227** - Mike Kemp/Getty Images; **p. 228** - Michael Rosskothen/Shutterstock; **pp. 230-231** - Mark Garlick/Science Photo Library/Getty Images; **pp. 232-233** - Mark Stevenson/Stocktrek Images/Getty Images; **p. 237** - Roman Garcia Mora; **p. 238** - The Natural History Museum/Alamy Stock Photo.

COVER: Herschel Hoffmeyer/Shutterstock
BACK COVER: Daniel Eskridge/Shutterstock

union square kids
NEW YORK

UNION SQUARE KIDS and the distinctive Union Square Kids logo are
trademarks of Union Square & Co., LLC.

Union Square & Co., LLC, is a subsidiary of Sterling Publishing Co., Inc.

© 2021 White Star s.r.l.

All rights reserved. No part of this publication may be reproduced, stored in a retrieval system, or transmitted in any form or by any means (including electronic, mechanical, photocopying, recording, or otherwise) without prior written permission from the Publisher

ISBN 978-1-4549-4607-6

For information about custom editions, special sales, and premium purchases, please contact specialsales@unionsquareandco.com.

Printed and manufactured in China by
Leo Paper Products, Heshan, Guangdong

Lot #: 2 4 6 8 10 9 7 5 3 1
07/22

unionsquareandco.com

Translation: TperTradurre s.r.l.
Editing: Michele Suchomel-Casey

Graphic design and graphic layout by **BIANCO TANGERINE**

All illustrations are an artist's rendering that's not based on fact

AUTHORS

DIEGO MATTARELLI - Diego has a degree in Geological Sciences and Technologies from the University of Milan-Bicocca, and for almost 15 years he has dedicated himself to the widespread dissemination of science to education institutions and the general public, collaborating with various institutions. His greatest passion, however, is dinosa he started learning about paleontology by going to museums and exhibitions, eventually becoming a hands-on paleontologist as part of an international team that carried out excavation campaigns in North Africa sponsored by National Geographic Society. He participated in the recovery of the most complete dinosaur skeleton on the African continent, a *Spinosaurus*, which changed the current understanding of dinosaurs. The discovery was published in t April 2020 issue of *Nature*, one of the most important scientific journals in the world. He has also published various works; he coauthored a series of science textbooks for lower secondary schools and has authored and coauthored numerous scientific publications in various fields. He is also the professor of Mineralogy and Physics applied to Restoration at IED - Aldo Galli Academy of Fine Arts in Como, Italy.

EMANUELA PAGLIARI - Emanuela has a degree in Natural Sciences from the University of Milan and boasts mor than 15 years of experience in scientific dissemination, carried out at the Civic Natural History Museum in Milan, the Ulrico Hoepli Planetarium in Milan, and other institutions. She is an expert in designing fun learning activities in th of natural sciences and has coauthored various educational scientific publications.

CRISTINA BANFI - Cristina has a degree in Natural Sciences from the University of Milan, and her master's thesis w paleontology. She is a teacher and founding member of the Associazione Didattica Museale - ADM (1994) and ADMaic (2015), associations that are active in the field of teaching in museums and at exhibitions. She has been involved in sc communication and fun learning for over 30 years, collaborating on the organization and design of cultural events and training courses. She has contributed to numerous school textbooks and educational publications.

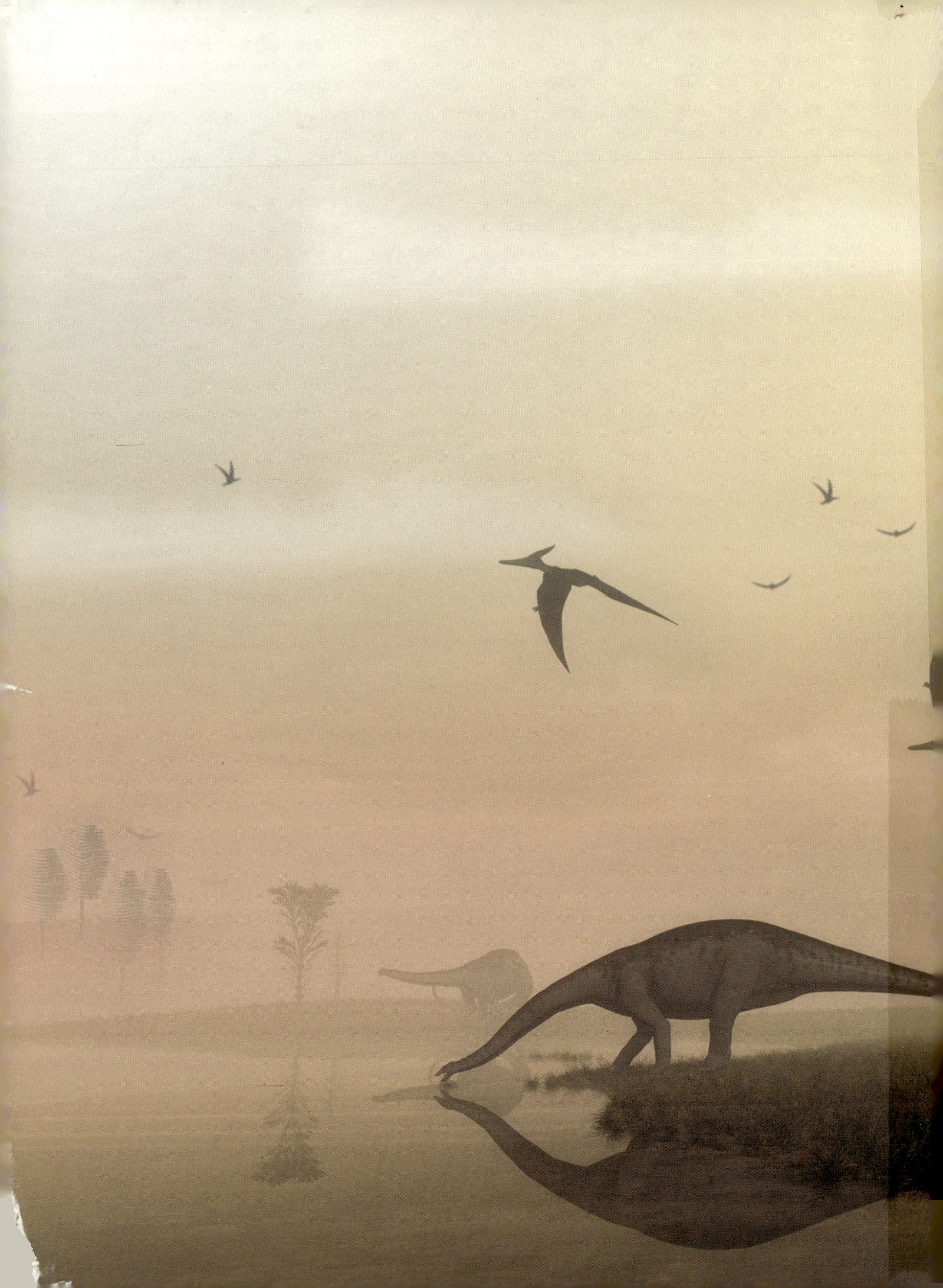